CULTURAL DIVERSITY IN THE PRIMARY SCHOOL

Education in a Multicultural Society

Series Editor: Maurice Craft
                Professor of Education
                University of Nottingham

Titles published:
THE MULTICULTURAL CURRICULUM
James Lynch

LANGUAGE IN MULTICULTURAL CLASSROOMS
Viv Edwards

HOME AND SCHOOL IN MULTICULTURAL BRITAIN
Sally Tomlinson

Cultural Diversity in the Primary School

David Houlton

B. T. Batsford Ltd
London

© David Houlton 1986
First published 1986

All rights reserved. No part of this publication
may be reproduced, in any form or by any means,
without permission from the Publisher

Typeset by Deltatype, Ellesmere Port
and printed in Great Britain by
Billings, Worcester

Published by B. T. Batsford Ltd
4 Fitzhardinge Street, London W1H 0AH

British Library Cataloguing in Publication Data

Houlton, David
    Cultural diversity in the primary school
    —— (Education in a multi-cultural society)
    I Education, Elementary —— Great Britain
    II Intercultural education —— Great Britain
    III Minorities —— Education (Elementary)
    —— Great Britain
    1. Title
    2. Series
    372'. 011'5   LA 6333
    ISBN 07134 4865 2

372

Primary schools. Sociological perspectives.
Multicultural education.

Contents

Acknowledgements

I am indebted to a number of colleagues who have offered advice and practical support at many points in the writing of this book. In particular I should like to single out Terry Alcott and Rena Cervi of the Rushey Mead Centre in Leicester, Professor Maurice Craft of the University of Nottingham, and Tony Seward of Batsford. Several colleagues have kindly allowed me to quote from their work, and to them I am very grateful: Janet Atkin of the University of Nottingham, Alma Craft of the School Curriculum Development Committee, Cherry Fulloway of Heather Brook Primary School, Leicester, Geneva Gay of the University of Purdue, Jim Green of Westdale Junior School, Nottingham, Alan James of Edge Hill College of Higher Education, Robin Richardson of Brent LEA, Stephen Rowland of the University of Sheffield, John Shearman of the Beeches Primary School, Peterborough, and John Twitchin of the BBC.

My thanks also to Jill Cleaver and Trish Docherty for so ably typing the manuscript and to Deborah Watchorn for making her graphic skills available. Finally, thanks are due to Sue, Claire and Thomas for tolerating yet more disruption to family life.

I should like to acknowledge the following who granted permission for the reproduction in the text of copyright materials: Edward Arnold and the School Curriculum Development Committee for the extracts from *All Our Languages*; BBC Publications for the extracts from *Multicultural Education: views from the classroom*; BBC-TV Continuing Education Dept. for the extracts from programmes in the series 'Case Studies in Multicultural Education'; Bell and Hyman for the extracts from Straker-Welds, M., *Education for a Multicultural Society: case studies in ILEA schools*; Harper and Row for the chart on page 80; London University Institute of Education for the Languages and Dialects Map on page 21; and Charles E. Merrill for the extracts from Rogers C., *Freedom to Learn for the 80s*.

David Houlton
Nottingham, May 1986

Editor's Preface

It is now coming to be more widely recognized that Britain is a culturally diverse society, and has been for centuries. Variations of belief and behaviour according to region, religion, class and ethnicity have always existed, but we are now increasingly conscious of the greater potential for enrichment – as well as for conflict – that these variations make possible. This series seeks to explore some of the more salient educational issues presented by cultural diversity, and with particular reference to *ethnicity*. It aims to contribute to the skills and understanding of teachers, teacher trainers, educational administrators and policymakers, whose concern is to provide for the educational needs of all children growing up in a multicultural society.

Cultural Diversity in the Primary School aims to introduce teachers of younger children to the particular opportunities and challenges of the infant and junior classroom, where so much subsequent behaviour is grounded. Drawing on his experience as a former inner-city primary school head, his extensive study of multilingual classrooms as Director of the Schools Council Mother Tongue Project, and his current work as a lecturer in primary education at Nottingham University, David Houlton presents multicultural and anti-racist teaching as an integral part of good primary practice. He offers a lively historical account of linguistic and cultural diversity in Britain, and his detailed exemplification of ideas, initiatives and resources will provide positive encouragement to teachers as they seek to respond to this diversity.

Maurice Craft
University of Nottingham

1 Thinking about diversity

Let us begin with two snapshots of teachers and children at work. The first involves Barbara Roberts, a teacher of nine- and ten-year-olds in a large multicultural primary school in Islington, North London. We join her when she and the children are discussing 'migration' and the reasons for people moving from one country to another:

T: For years and years people have been moving about, going to settle in different parts of the world. Remember I talked to you one day about the highlands of Scotland and how there aren't many people there now . . .

[She draws on her own experience as a Scot and talks about the clearance of people from the highlands and their migration to more southern areas. Then . . .]

T: Do any of you children know why your parents moved to this country?

P: My mum brought me here to have a better education.

P: My dad came here to find work.

P: Because of the soldiers . . . in Cyprus.

T: Yes, at one time there was a war in Cyprus . . . a lot of people sometimes have to move because of wars.

So we've got all these different countries represented here in our classroom and we've got people moving here from their own country for different reasons.

[Later, in an Art activity:]

T: I want you all to draw your hands . . . draw right round your hands with your fingers open . . .

Let's look closely at our hands. . . . Can you see all the different skin tones?

When you are painting your picture I want you to try to get . . . as near as possible the same colour as you see on your hands . . . you can experiment with mixing all the different colours together and when you think you've got the colour I want you to paint your hands.

[On another occasion:]

T: What accent have I got?

P: A Scottish accent.

T: I've got a Scottish accent. Accent is the way I speak and it's part of my personality.

Another way that people bring a different kind of language with them when they move is that sometimes they speak with a different dialect. [There follows a dialogue in Jamaican dialect between two girls.]

T: Then we come to people who . . . are speaking an entirely different kind of language.
[A group of boys read aloud a Turkish story and translate it into English.]

T: Does anyone know the word for someone who can speak two languages? . . . It's bilingual . . . You're very, very clever if somebody says that you're bilingual.[1]

For the second example we move further north to Leicestershire where children from the rural Newbold Verdon Primary School are taking part in a series of exchange visits with Shaftesbury, an inner city multicultural school. The children have been involved in activities around the Hindu festival, Divali.

[They and their teachers are here talking about the project:]

P: They've got their religions and although they've got more gods our god is all their gods into one.

P: When we went to the sari shop that lady said she only believed in one god . . . the goddess of wealth. So really it's just that they've got many gods but some people just choose one.
[Later the discussion turns to questions of language:]

P: They seemed to be speaking in their own language when they got together on their own but when they came up to us and that they spoke in English.

T: Did you ask them to speak in their language?

P: Yes, but they wouldn't do it.

T: Why?

P: In case we thought it would be funny . . . we might think it was a bit queer.

P: One of the boys in our group was a Muslim . . . Muslim . . . and he spoke . . . er . . .

T: Gujarati, was it?

P: Yes, Gujarati.

P: He spoke Punjabi and he was Muslim religion.[2]

In different ways these two sets of teachers are bringing to their curriculum an awareness of the culturally diverse society in which their pupils are growing up. Their choice of starting points differs since the classes they are working with have very different ethnic make-ups and the children themselves come from different sorts of communities.

Barbara Roberts is essentially concerned, like many teachers in multicultural classrooms, with giving validity and recognition to her pupils' languages, cultures and sense of ethnicity. The Leicestershire teachers, on the other hand, have set themselves the task of helping their children to look outwards from the cultural world of the village where they live in order to better appreciate the diversity of the wider community. What both groups of teachers have in common, however, is that they are aiming to equip children with, in the words of the Swann Report,[3] 'the knowledge, understanding and skills' for living in today's multicultural Britain and, in the process of doing this, are revising their own assumptions about what this knowledge should comprise and what these skills should consist of.

Fifteen years ago, approaches of the sort just described would have been virtually impossible to find, commonplace as they may be nowadays. Twenty years ago they would have been non-existent. They have evolved as British society has become more visibly a multicultural one. As families from other parts of the world, most notably the former Empire, have uprooted themselves to escape poverty, hunger, war or repression, or have responded to calls to bring their labour to the 'motherland', the composition of Britain has changed. And gradually teachers have begun to acknowledge the implications of these changes in the curriculum they offer to children.

If as teachers we look back over our own professional development and our growing awareness of the multicultural society in which we find ourselves it is likely that, for many of us, the impetus for reviewing the content of our curricula and the assumptions we make about what children should learn will have come from the fact that we have had daily contact with children whose families and communities have their origins and cultural roots in other parts of the world. Underlying this is a tendency for us to see Britain's conversion to a multicultural society as being a recent occurrence, stretching back no further than, say, the early 1950s. Furthermore, we tend to assume that before these post-war influxes of other ethnic groups Britain was to all intents and purposes a culturally homogeneous society with a common set of values, sense of history and culture, and a unifying common language. Nothing could be further from the truth. Indeed, these islands have a long tradition of cultural diversity stretching back over many centuries. Irish communities were established in London and the West Coast ports as long ago as 1400. Accounts dating from the thirteenth century record hostility towards Jewish communities. Italian workers were recruited by Edward VI on account of their armour-making skills, and Elizabeth I's ministers sent to Italy for alum-makers for the weaving industry.[4] Post-war immigration, then, has been the latest phase of a developing and complex cultural mosaic.

Unfortunately this historical dimension to our thinking about cultural diversity has been much neglected. I therefore want to offer at this early stage in our discussion a more detailed picture than the one that has been available to us up until now. Language will figure quite prominently in this picture. But this is not to suggest that language has been the sole source of diversity. Religion, too, has played a prominent part. And in today's Britain social class and regional factors are important influences on the diversity around us. At this stage, however, I am choosing to give some emphasis to linguistic differences since these are indicators of broader variation in attitude and behaviour. It is through their languages that all ethnic groups develop a sense of corporate identity and transmit their culture and values to the rising generation.[5] Equally, through looking at the way a society uses language we can learn a great deal about how power is distributed and the role that language plays in maintaining positions of power – important issues in any discussion of multicultural education.

The 'older' languages of Britain

Our knowledge of the older linguistic pattern of Britain is by no means complete, but thanks to writers such as Glanville Price[6] and W. B. Lockwood[7] a clearer picture is beginning to emerge. For an overview of what has gone on we can turn initially to Glanville Price:[8]

> In the late prehistoric times the Celts were everywhere . . . There were the enigmatic Picts. Then the Romans came, but Latin never took root here as it did in mainland provinces of the [Roman] empire.
>
> The Romans left and were succeeded by the English, whose speech spread . . . submerging the languages of later arrivals, Norse (which however survived for nearly 1000 years in the Northern Isles) and Anglo-Norman (but not without being profoundly influenced by it in its vocabulary), displacing the traditional French of the Channel Islands . . .

To this we should add that, despite the relentless progress of English we know that Cornish, which expired two centuries ago, and Manx which disappeared in very recent years, are now both the subjects of revival movements. Irish survives in the Republic of Ireland and to a degree in Northern Ireland, too. Scottish Gaelic has been maintained in the Northern and Western Isles. Romani has been around for over 500 years. And Welsh, after much erosion at the hands of the English, is now showing signs of renewed vigour.

The Celtic languages

The earliest Britons would have spoken a Celtic language, which would probably have been an early form of Welsh. In fact, Welsh is the oldest living language in Europe. In its early forms it pre-dates the Roman conquest by two or even three centuries. It also has the longest literary tradition of any European language: one that remains unbroken to the present day. And, most relevant to the theme of this chapter, the language continues to occupy a central position in the lives and cultural identities of many children and their families.

The struggle for Welsh has been a bitter one. Its story of decline, and the role played by English-speaking authorities, is well-chronicled. One of the more graphic accounts, which has striking parallels with the situation of our more recently arrived languages, is to be found in Richard Llewelyn's *How Green Was My Valley*:

> I heard crying in the infants' school, as though a child had fallen . . . a small girl came through the door and walked a couple of steps towards us . . .
>
> About her neck a piece of new cord, and from the cord, a board that hung to her shins and cut her as she walked. Chalked on the board . . . 'I must not speak Welsh at school' . . . And the board dragged her down, for she was small, an infant, and the cord rasped the flesh of her neck, and there were marks upon her shins where the edge of the board had cut. Loud she cried, with a rise and fall in the tone, . . . and in her eyes the big tears of a child who is in hurt, and has shame, and is frightened.[9]

That the decline has now been arrested and hostility to the language reduced must largely be attributable to the introduction of Welsh-medium teaching in schools and colleges and the passing of the 1967 Welsh Language Act with the resulting increase in the use of Welsh in public affairs.

Irish, too, was well-established by the time the Romans arrived in Britain. Yet sadly the succeeding centuries reveal a steady decline, accelerated in the seventeenth century with the 'plantation' of English settlers and the beginning of the long economic and political domination by London. Despite this, even in the most anglicized areas, there are numerous seventeenth and eighteenth century reports of attempts to keep the language alive through poetry and cultural activities, and of ministers preaching in Irish to their congregations.[10] As late as 1880 we are told that fairs were often a time for people to come together in the North and converse in Irish. Since partition in 1920 some members of the Ulster Catholic minority have taken the language to their hearts and have made it, as well as its accompanying poetry, music and dance traditions, the focus for a determined maintenance movement – one that is steadily gaining momentum in the cities of the English mainland.

The earliest surviving Scottish Gaelic text dates from the twelfth century. At this time Gaelic was almost certainly the principal language of the Scottish mainland, Orkney and Shetland having been predominantly Norse-speaking since the Viking invasions of AD 800. English influence began to be felt in the lowland areas and gradually came to dominate Scottish political life, a fact which generated much resistance among the Highlanders and stiffened their resolve to maintain Gaelic. Evidence of their effectiveness was seen in the late seventeenth century when the Church of Scotland announced that in order to 'exercise its ministry' in the Highlands it would need to work through the medium of Gaelic to ensure an adequate supply of Gaelic speaking ministers.[11] Nevertheless decline continued. In recent years, however, a strong revival movement, especially in the Western Isles, has given the language a new stability.[12]

Only in 1974 did Manx, the language of the Isle of Man, become extinct. It was then that Ned Mandrell, the last surviving native speaker, died at the age of 97. The origins of the language go back to the fourth or fifth centuries when the Gaels arrived in Man from Ireland. Its strength in the ensuing centuries is beyond doubt. As late as the nineteenth century, preaching in the language was widespread. In 1874 it was estimated that 30 per cent of the population spoke the language habitually. Today, though technically extinct, the language lives on through a revival campaign and also in the local spoken English through numerous everyday expressions, place names and family names.

Cornish, too, is techically extinct in the sense that it has no surviving native speakers, the last one, Dolly Pentreath, having died in 1777 in her late 80s. Like other languages already mentioned Cornish also has its roots in the Celtic tongues which were spoken in Britain before the Roman invasion. As a living language it probably reached its peak in the tenth century when Cornwall enjoyed some independence from the rest of Britain. From then onwards the story is a familiar one of deterioration. Even so, as late as the mid-seventeenth century there are records of church services being presented in the language. The final death knell seems to have tolled about 1800[13] as Cornish ports rose in importance, encouraging the 'immigration' of English speakers from other parts of Britain. Moves to revive the language are unlikely ever to be on the same scale as those associated with Welsh and Gaelic but since 1967 the Cornish Language Board has been in existence and organizes evening classes, plays, readings, and occasional publications.

Later arrivals

Latin was introduced to Britain with the invasion of Claudius in 43 AD, and remained in official use until some time after the withdrawal of the Roman legions 500 years later. To what extent it was adopted by the population at large is difficult to ascertain but there is no evidence that it actually supplanted the indigenous Celtic languages. What seems most likely is that it became the *lingua franca* in the more Romanized towns of the South East but that nevertheless a great deal of bilingualism in the country as a whole was retained. Latin certainly became the language of 'law, government, business and cultured life',[14] and so, as one might expect, many non-native speakers chose to cultivate it for purposes of social prestige. With the advent of the Normans in 1066 the language inevitably began to decline, but not dramatically, as for some years it continued to be employed for many official purposes and remained a strong influence in education.

However, it is in the language of the Angles, Saxons and Jutes who arrived here around 410 AD from the Low Countries and Germany that we find the foundation of modern English. Over the ensuing years the language gained ground rapidly, and though suffering something of a setback with the expanding influence of French following the Norman Conquest, by the twelfth century it had come into its own again and eventually, with its many regional characteristics, became the language as we know it today.

While English was gaining its foothold in the Midlands and the South East, another more ancient language was still in active use in the far North of Britain. Norse, the language of the Vikings, had taken root in Orkney and Shetland as a result of the Norwegian invasion of the eighth century. From the same time the Danish Vikings had begun to install themselves further south and by the middle of the ninth century had taken York, transforming it into a Norse-speaking city. Evidence of the language's influence throughout other parts of Britain remains today, especially in the names of villages, towns, islands and rivers.[15] It was in the far north, however, that Norse took its most enduring hold. As late as 1700 the Reverend John Brand[16] reported of Orkney: . . . 'there are some who speak Norse . . . there are a few yet living who can speak no other thing'. Languages decline for many reasons, but Murdoch Mackenzie writing in 1750 provides a salutary explanation for the demise of Norse which gives food for thought for us today:

> . . . thirty or forty years ago this (Norse) was the vulgar language of two parishes: since which, by means of Charity Schools, it is so much wore out, as to be understood by none but the old . . .[17]

So, over two hundred years ago, the alarm bells were being rung: without positive encouragement from schools the languages, and therefore the cultures of minority communities, may cease to exist.

Before completing this linguistic survey of Britain's past, a few other languages need to be mentioned.

It is not difficult to imagine how the feelings of the Saxons and indigenous Britons would have run high when, in the aftermath of the Norman Conquest, their own languages came under attack as the French-speaking minority, never more than about 5 per cent of the population, began to occupy positions of power out of all proportion to their numbers. The situation has been summed up by Orr[18] as follows:

> French is spoken practically everywhere. It is the language of the court and

society, it is the language of administration, of Parliament, and of the law courts, it is the language of church and monastery, it is taught and spoken in schools, where English is forbidden.

One effect of this Norman domination was an increase in bilingualism as, for purposes of social survival, many people gradually began to acquire a knowledge of French as a second language.

Yet, even when French had declined and English had ridden into the ascendancy, it continued to be the language of court until 1399, the year that saw the accession of Henry IV as the first monarch since 1066 to have English as a mother tongue. After such a period of dominance it is little surprise that the language should have left its mark on English, on a scale far greater than we sometimes realize: Baugh and Cable[19] have estimated that, between the twelfth and fifteenth centuries, about 10,000 French words found their way into English and 75 per cent remain in common use today.

German has been quite a significant language in different parts of Britain. During Elizabeth I's reign 3,838 Germans were counted in London alone.[20] Pressure on Germans to assimilate, however, seems to have been quite strong, for many chose to Anglicize their names – Schmid became Smith, Steinhaus was changed to Stonehouse and Roth became Rudd. Even so, by 1800, Nemnich was able to find German communities in Hull, Liverpool, Leeds and Glasgow and set the London German population at 30,000.

Dutch speakers were numerous in East Anglia and the South East ports from the early fourteenth century. By the early 1600s the Kent port of Sandwich was being described as 'transformed into a Flemish town'.[21] And by 1580 Dutch speakers represented one third of the population of Norwich.

Finally, we must mention Romani, the language of the Gypsies, whose movements and emigration can be traced back to eleventh century India. It is not known precisely when the language and its people first made an appearance in Britain, but in the mid-sixteenth century, Elizabeth's civil servants were estimating the Gypsy population of England to be 10,000. The language has undergone many changes over the years and today there is some debate as to whether in its modern form it is comparable with the 'deep Romani' of the last century and earlier.[22] That the language continues to flourish, however, is beyond question – only now its function is not so much that of a mother tongue but rather a 'secret language'[23] used as a means of identifying other Gypsies and maintaining a sense of group identity. Acton and Davies[24] have estimated at least 50,000 speakers in England and Wales, a figure that seems likely to be maintained now that a start has been made on teaching the language to children.

So far there has been a strong linguistic theme to the discussion. We have seen something of the interplay that took place between different languages, how they borrowed from each other and how evidence of them can still be seen in the present day English language. Also we have been able to draw some parallels between the treatment meted out to the languages, especially by schools and official bodies, and the situation of today's minority language communities. That leads us into thinking about the ethnic groups who form the major part of our present day multicultural society. It has already been pointed out that Irish people, the largest ethnic minority in Britain, have been settled here for over 600 years. Similarly with the Italians and other white minorities. But what about black people?

Black People in Britain

The first contact that the British are likely to have had with black people was during the period 193–211 AD when the Roman emperor ruling England was a man of North African origin, Septimius Severus. Later, in the third century, we learn from Fryer[25] of a 'division of Moors' in the Roman army based in Britain. Further contact with black people would have taken place in the Middle East during the Crusades of the twelfth and thirteenth centuries. In the ensuing years the growing trade in African gold through the Mediterranean and the Muslim occupation of Spain would almost certainly have led black people to settle in Britain.

Documentation becomes more reliable and detailed in the sixteenth century when the developing sea trade with West Africa resulted in traders such as John Locke bringing to England 'certain black slaves whereof some were tall and strong men',[26] in order to sell them for household use.

This trade in human cargo was given royal approval when, in 1652, Queen Elizabeth sponsored Sir John Hawkins to transport slaves from West Africa to the New World. Gradually, then, black people became a more common sight in English towns but it was not long before the prejudices of the day led to demands for their expulsion. Elizabeth's voice joined the public clamour and resulted in the issuing of 'an especial commandment that the said kind of people be with all speed . . . discharged out of . . . her majesty's dominion.'[27] This growing 'race phobia', as Nigel File and Chris Power[28] have called it, was a recurring theme throughout the seventeenth and eighteenth centuries, and by 1764 a writer in the *Gentleman's Magazine* was complaining about there being 20,000[29] 'negroe servants' in London (this, according to contemporary estimates, out of a population of about 676,000). Even at this time, some of the stereotyped characteristics to which we

have become well-accustomed in more recent years were being
ascribed to the black population: '[they] are generally sullen, spiteful,
treacherous and revengeful'.[30] Towards the end of the eighteenth
century calls for expulsion were again being heard. In the words of one
writer, the country was becoming 'a refuge for all the blacks who chose
to come here' and, he went on, 'if the legislature did not take some
method to prevent the introduction of any more . . . London would, in
another century, have the appearance of an Ethiopian colony'.[31] In the
ninteenth century there are accounts[32,33] of several black people who,
each in their own way, made an important contribution to some field of
human endeavour in Britain. There is William Cuffay who was born of
a St Kitts slave, yet became a leading Chartist and suffered for his
political convictions by being transported to Tasmania. The
Jamaican-born 'forgotten nurse',[34] Mary Seacole, served in the thick
of the fighting in the Crimea, nursing the British wounded. There is the
composer Samuel Coleridge-Taylor who campaigned unstintingly
against the racism that he met in Britain at the turn of the century and,
through his music, worked to promote Black identity. Accounts now
exist of numerous other black men and women who, throughout the
nineteenth and early twentieth centuries, made significant contributions to medicine, politics, science and the arts.[35]

Although the examples quoted so far have a predominantly Afro-
Caribbean theme, there are many parallels among people from Asian
and European backgrounds who have settled here. For instance, there
was the Gujarati-speaking Dadabhai Nairoji who, in 1892, was elected
as Britain's first black MP. He represented the Finsbury Central
constituency until 1895 and during his period of office associated
himself with many progressive measures such as Home Rule for
Ireland, women's suffrage and trade union rights.[36]

From about 1870 onwards it was common for students from British
colonies to come to Britain in order to further their studies. Indeed,
there are a number of contemporary accounts of the 'attitudes of
superiority' shown towards them by the indigenous population.[37] The
universities themselves were often no more enlightened in their
attitudes. This is strongly testified by the tales of racial discrimination
that figure in the autobiography of D. F. Karaka who, in the early part
of this century, was the first black person to be elected President of the
Oxford Union.[38]

As far as the vast majority of ethnic minority people are concerned,
who came to Britain at the end of the last century and in the early years
of the present one, however, there is little record of their lives and
experiences apart from those which live on in the memories of friends
and relatives. For many of these people the First World War was a

major landmark as it created an unprecedented demand for labour which resulted in black and other minority workers being brought to Britain either as merchant seamen or as labourers for the ordnance factories. Many returned home at the end of the war but others stayed on and, as seafarers, settled in the dockland areas of the major ports – London, Liverpool, Bristol, Manchester and elsewhere, including Cardiff's Tiger Bay which, as the subject of a programme in the Channel 4 series 'Struggle for Black Community',[39] provides us with graphic accounts of the lives of black people living at the time. That they were not received with hospitality is illustrated by several contributors' recollections of the 1919 'race riots', summed up in the following epitaph that appears in English and Urdu on a Cardiff gravestone:

> In loving memory of Mohammed Abdullah who was killed in the riots of June 12, 1919, Age 21 years.[40]

There are references in the programme to the disproportionate levels of unemployment experienced by black people and we hear that discrimination existed even in the payment of unemployment benefits. A former engine room worker recalls:

> When the white man was getting 17s and 6d a week the black man was only getting 15s for unemployment benefit . . . we fought for the same level.[41]

The contributors to the television programme were in no doubt about the sacrifices they had made for Britain, not least in times of war:

> We have spilt blood for this country. In 1939 the docks were like something in Ancient Egypt: one out of every black family was killed . . . Children torpedoed at the age of 14. Lost on their first sortie over Germany at 18 years of age. Going to Canada to train to be pilots. When people like the National Front tell me 'We fought to keep this country great', I don't even have to mention the King's Own African Rifles or the Gurkhas. What I mention is the contribution made by this area to that struggle. The number of Somali, West African, West Indian and Arab seamen without families who went down. Their names cannot be recorded. But of the people who had families, one in every family was lost.[42]

Lest we should think that this is simply a chapter of history and has little relevance for the present generation, we now hear from young adults who see very clearly the parallels between the experience of their grandparents and their own lives today:

> We had seen Powell's speech in '65 which changed the whole dialogue about race. Then the '68 and '71 Acts. I have a feeling . . . we were being put in the same position as the people in 1919. Blacks were being blamed for all the problems of social deprivation that were around . . . we were beginning to re-write our own history.[43]

When I was younger I spent a lot of time with my grandmother and the older members of my family . . . That stood me in really good stead for when I came across racism because I grew up with the memories of race riots and the struggles that our grandparents went through: what it was like for a white woman, married to a black man, bringing up children. My grandmother had impressed on me that I am what I am and that I didn't have to bend a knee to anybody.[44]

Diversity Today

To complete our picture, then, let us draw together some of the data available to us on the composition of present day British society. The 1971 Census gives details of the overseas-born population by country of origin. The data show that, of a total population of nearly 54 million, a little over three million people were born overseas. More than half a million were of West Indian origin, mostly Jamaican, and something less than half a million were born in South Asia. Approximately one third of a million originated from Africa, the Far East and the Mediterranean, and a further half million came from Europe. The latest census, in 1981, did not collect information on country of origin but the 1981 Labour Survey showed that of 12 million heads of households 11.4 per cent had their origin outside the UK, the majority originating in the Caribbean or Indian sub-continent.

A Department of Education and Science (DES) survey of all 104 local education authorities (LEAs) was conducted in 1982 as part of an investigation into the response to the EEC Directive on the Education of Children of Migrant Workers.[45] This revealed that, of the total UK school population aged between 5 and 16, approximately 4 per cent (375,000) of children live in families where English is not the first language. However it has been estimated elsewhere that this may be a conservative figure, a truer estimate being over 500,000.[46] Because of the absence of a specific 'ethnic' or language question in the 1981 Census it is difficult to arrive at precise figures on the size of particular language groups. Nevertheless some estimates are available and further help is provided by language surveys conducted in different parts of the country. The team of writers responsible for producing the Children's Language Project,[47] have estimated that in Britain in 1981 there were well over one million speakers of South Asian languages, mainly Bengali, Gujarati, Hindi, Kutchi, Punjabi and Urdu. They estimated speakers of the other major languages as totalling: Arabic (100,000), Chinese (140,000), Greek Cypriots (120,000), Turkish Cypriots (30,000), Italians (180,000), Polish (130,000), Ukrainian (30,000), Portuguese (30,000) and Spanish (50,000). To help demonstrate the dispersal of these and other languages throughout the UK the same writers produced a simple linguistic map (Figure 1).[48]

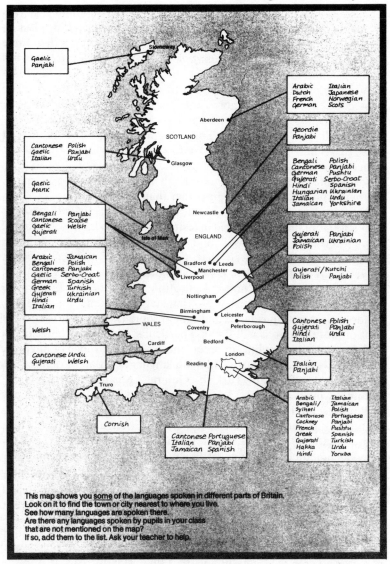

The following labels appear on the map:

Gaelic
Panjabi

Arabic   Italian
Dutch   Japanese
French   Norwegian
German   Scots

Cantonese   Polish
Gaelic   Panjabi
Italian   Urdu

Geordie
Panjabi

Gaelic
Manx

Bengali   Polish
Cantonese   Panjabi
German   Pushtu
Gujerati   Serbo-Croat
Hindi   Spanish
Hungarian   Ukrainian
Italian   Urdu
Jamaican   Yorkshire

Bengali   Panjabi
Cantonese   Scouse
Gaelic   Welsh
Gujerati

Gujerati   Panjabi
Jamaican   Ukrainian
Polish

Arabic   Jamaican
Bengali   Polish
Cantonese   Panjabi
Gaelic   Serbo-Croat
German   Spanish
Greek   Turkish
Gujerati   Ukrainian
Hindi   Urdu
Italian

Gujerati / Kutchi
Polish   Panjabi

Welsh

Cantonese   Polish
Gujerati   Panjabi
Hindi   Urdu
Italian

Cantonese Urdu
Gujerati   Welsh

Italian
Panjabi

Cornish

Cantonese Portuguese
Italian   Panjabi
Jamaican   Spanish

Arabic   Italian
Bengali/   Jamaican
Sylheti   Polish
Cantonese   Portuguese
Cockney   Panjabi
French   Pushtu
Greek   Spanish
Gujerati   Turkish
Hakka   Urdu
Hindi   Yoruba

Map cities: Stornoway, Aberdeen, SCOTLAND, Glasgow, Newcastle, Isle of Man, ENGLAND, Bradford, Leeds, Manchester, Liverpool, Nottingham, Birmingham, Leicester, Coventry, Peterborough, WALES, Cardiff, Bedford, London, Reading, Truro

This map shows you some of the languages spoken in different parts of Britain.
Look on it to find the town or city nearest to where you live.
See how many languages are spoken there.
Are there any languages spoken by pupils in your class
that are not mentioned on the map?
If so, add them to the list. Ask your teacher to help.

Figure 1
CHILDREN'S LANGUAGE PROJECT

Notice how the map also includes some of the indigenous varieties of English, for example, Scouse, Geordie and Cockney. For these writers would stress that although one of our starting points for thinking about cultural diversity in schools would be with languages other than

English spoken by ethnic minority children, in fact all pupils in a class are likely to have quite wide linguistic repertoires, including class or regional dialects of English which will often constitute their own mother tongues and thereby their links with the culture and traditions of their families and communities.

A survey of primary schools by the Schools Council Mother Tongue Project[49] helps us to focus more closely on children in school. Of the 92 LEAs returning questionnaires, almost two thirds had at least one school with over 10 per cent bilingual pupils.[50] Just over one third of these LEAs had between one and ten schools in this category, and just under two-thirds had between 11 and 85. Altogether the LEAs reported a total of 1,892 primary schools where at least 10 per cent of the pupils have a mother tongue other than English.

More in-depth information about patterns of linguistic diversity is available from the several local investigations which have been carried out in recent years. Rosen and Burgess'[51] study of 28 London secondary schools, showed that 14 per cent of the 4,600 pupils surveyed were bilingual, speaking 55 different languages between them, whilst the Inner London Education Authority's (ILEA's) 1983 Language Census[52] recorded 147 languages spoken by school age children. It is not unusual to find that in some London schools 75 per cent or more of pupils will speak a particular community language in addition to English, whilst in others there is a wider range of linguistic variation with the authority's 12 main languages (in order of numbers of speakers) – Bengali, Turkish, Gujarati, Spanish, Greek, Urdu, Punjabi, Chinese, Italian, Arabic, French and Portuguese – all being well represented among pupils.[53]

But by far the most extensive survey of language diversity was carried out in 1980–81 by the Linguistic Minorities Project (LMP).[54] This documented the range of languages in use among school age children in five LEAs: Bradford, Coventry, Haringey, Peterborough and Waltham Forest (Table 1).[55]

There are several points of interest for us in these findings. The number of languages in use is quite dramatic: we would expect to see the main South Asian languages featuring prominently but the presence of Southern and Eastern European languages might well come as a surprise, reminding us that linguistic diversity is often as strong among white minorities as among others. Each of the LEAs has

Table 1. *Language diversity among schoolchildren in five LEAs* (adapted from the Linguistic Minorities Project)

LEAs	Number of pupils using a language other than English	Percentage of pupils using a language other than English	Number of identifiably distinct languages reported	Most frequently reported spoken languages or language grouping expressed as % of number of pupils using a language other than English
Bradford	14,201	17.8	64	Punjabi(53) Urdu(19) Gujarati(9) Bengali(3) Pushtu(3) Italian(3) Polish(1) Hindi(1) Chinese(1) Creoles(1) Ukrainian(1)
Coventry	7,189	14.4	50	Punjabi(59) Gujarati(16) Urdu(7) Hindi(3) Italian(2) Bengali(2) Polish(2) Chinese(1) Creoles(1)
Haringey	7,407	30.7	87	Greek(34) Turkish(15) Creoles(9) Gujarati(6) Italian(6) French-based Creoles(4) Bengali(3) Urdu(2) Punjabi(2) Spanish(2) Chinese(2) French(1)
Peterborough	2,408	7.4	42	Punjabi(24) Italian(24) Urdu(18) Gujarati(12) Chinese(4) Polish(2) German(2) Hindi(2) Creoles(1) French(1)
Waltham Forest	5,521	18.8	65	Punjabi(31) Urdu(21) Gujarati(8) Greek(8) Creoles(7) Turkish(4) French-based Creoles(3) Bengali(3) Chinese(2) Italian(2) Hindi(1) French(1)

quite significant numbers of Creole speakers, another dimension of pupils' linguistic resources which is often overlooked in schools. Finally the LMP's findings, along with those of the other surveys we have mentioned, call into question the long-held assumption that as more ethnic minority children are born in Britain and grow up regarding themselves as British so the traditional languages of their communities will fall into disuse and cease to have any real function in their lives. Obviously there is a tendency for the English language to dominate and for this dominance to increase but it is worth noting that in both the Rosen and LMP surveys almost half of the children studied reported some literacy facility in their languages. Furthermore in recent years there has been quite a dramatic increase in the number of children attending community-run classes and, indeed, in the provision which communities themselves are making for linguistic and cultural maintenance. The net effect of all this, as many primary teachers will now testify, is that diversity is becoming more prominent among children and thereby a more compelling classroom agenda item than at any other time.

School Responses to Diversity

Although cultural diversity has long been a part of life in Britain it is only in the past 20 years or so that any serious consideration has been given to the implications that it poses for policy and practice in schools. Several writers have attached their own labels to the main lines of development. Gerry Davis[56] suggests that most types of practice can be grouped under four main headings:

1. Treat them all the same
2. Special needs
3. Compensatory model
4. Curriculum with multicultural aspects.

Davis's typology can be taken as a starting point from which to examine some of the other perspectives that abound at the present time and, thereby, reach a more concise statement than has been possible so far.

Treat them all the same was for some years the prevailing philosophy of teachers in many primary schools with children from different cultural backgrounds. It stemmed from a belief that by 'treating them all the same', in other words playing down differences in culture and skin colour, the teacher would be helping children to live harmoniously together and to appreciate the common experiences which bind them together as human beings rather than the differences which, if emphasized, could divide them from each other and set them apart from the mainstream society. In practice, it usually means that all children are treated as though they are white and Anglo Saxon, living their lives according to the norms of some unitary British culture. There are many problems with this assumption. Is there, indeed, a homogeneous British culture to which all members of the white British-born population would unanimously subscribe? Probably not. Among indigenous Britons there is considerable cultural and linguistic variation, based on regional and class affiliation. Increasingly there are people who have shied away from a traditional English life-style linked to Christian values, beliefs and norms of family life. And, as Michael Hussey reminds us,[57] there are many hybrid individuals whose styles of living are influenced 'by a number of cultures – Chinese cuisine, European classical music, African art, Russian literature and Hindu philosophy'. So 'treating them all the same' is likely to entail the teacher in making curriculum selections from a knowledge system which for large sections of the population holds little significance or meaning. This monocultural approach also raises a major ethical question: is it morally acceptable to treat a group of people as if each member is exactly the same when patently each is very different from each other? The effect of doing so is far reaching: it restricts minority children's access to the knowledge systems of their own communities and thereby may reinforce any prevailing messages which they have already absorbed about the social worth of their ethnic group and culture; whilst for other children it does little to equip them with the knowledge and skills necessary for living among cultural forms other than those with which they have been brought up. The Swann report sums this up well:

> . . . a failure to broaden the perspectives represented to all pupils – particularly those from the ethnic majority community – through their education not only leaves them inadequately prepared for adult life but also constitutes a fundamental mis-education, in failing to reflect the diversity which is now a fact of life in this country.[58]

The special needs approach argues that ethnic minority children have certain special needs deriving from the fact that many come from home cultures where a language other than English is the main medium of communication. An overriding priority, then, is for tuition in English as a Second Language (ESL) in order to equip the child to cope with the day-to-day demands of the classroom and to communicate effectively in the wider society. By comparison, any other needs such as cultural maintenance or support for the home language are thought to be of lesser importance.

Whilst few of us would dispute the necessity of ESL provision we have gradually come to recognize that ESL teachers actually perform more than a language teaching function: they help to socialize the child into the norms, values and cultural system of the school. And if this teaching takes place without careful regard to the cultural being of the child and the value system and code of behaviour which he or she has grown up to know in the home it can not only serve to confuse the child's developing self-image but also, by omission, devalue those aspects of life which he or she associates distinctly with the home. It was to these dangers that the Bullock report was alluding when it exhorted that 'no child should be expected to cast off the language and culture of the home' on entering school 'nor to live and act as though school and home represent two totally separate and different cultures'.[59]

In more recent years it has been interesting to see how the special needs argument has broadened slightly in order to accommodate more of the cultural world that the child knows and, recently, the mother tongue. Important as these are, however, we should ask ourselves whether they are the exclusive possession of the ethnic minority child or whether, as the Swann report maintains, they should be part of every child's learning agenda, components of a 'new education for all'.[60]

Growing out of this latter development we have the *compensatory* approach which sought to modify the normal curriculum in the direction of the ethnic minority child by injecting doses of cultural relevance. In secondary schools this trend gave rise to the 'Black Studies' and 'Asian Studies' movements of the 1970s, whilst at primary level the same philosophy underpinned the offering to ethnic minority children of culturally appropriate topic work – a project on India for instance, or classes in Indian dance and cookery. As Gerry Davis points out, it was as though ethnic minority children 'were being compensated for being deficient white children'.[61] In essence, the approach was a separatist one, its inherent dangers being summed up by the Report of the Parliamentary Select Committee when it warned against creating 'an educational ghetto for black pupils'.[62] The approach did little towards acquainting all children with the depth and richness of each other's cultures. It left the fundamental premises of the curriculum intact and unquestioned. And, not surprisingly, ethnic minority communities were quick to recognize its limitations. Indeed many felt their reservations to have been voiced succinctly by Salman Rushdie when, in a 1982 Channel Four broadcast, he said: 'And now there's a new catchword – "multiculturalism". In our schools, this means little more than teaching the kids a few bongo rhythms and how to tie a sari . . . Multiculturalism is the latest token gesture towards Britain's blacks. It ought to be exposed – like "integration" and "racial harmony" – for the sham it is.'[63]

The fourth model is the *curriculum with multicultural aspects*. Labelled by Lynch as an 'additive' tactic[64] this calls for the insertion of small components of the ethnic minority child's culture into the curriculum already on offer, or rather those sections of it like art, RE, music and drama which are considered to be most amenable to influence. Significantly, substantial other areas of knowledge, most notably maths, science and English, remain unaffected. The only conclusion that can be reasonably drawn from this clear line of demarcation is that a multicultural infusion into the curriculum is acceptable but only in so far as it is confined to the more peripheral 'soft' areas of knowledge, whilst the 'hard' cognitive domains – the 'basics' of learning – continue much as they have done.[65] Inevitably we here have a recipe for superficiality as far as the curriculum treatment of minority cultural experiences is concerned. As this writer has stated on previous occasions, the ethnic minority child's life comprises 'an intricate tapestry of cultural experiences . . . with its own values, expectations, norms of behaviour and modes of communication . . . Any curriculum acknowledgement of the child's culture must take account of this complexity and be more than a superficial study of its surface features. It needs to go further than promoting diversity at the level of . . . "clothing, calypsos, cooking and customs", or what I heard a headteacher recently describe as the 3-S syndrome – "sarees, samosas and steelbands" '.[66]

In reviewing these perspectives on the curriculum many of us will be able to chart the development of our own thinking and practice. Certainly I can recall my own progression in the 1970s from a special needs emphasis to an approach based on making multicultural insertions into key areas of my classroom practice. And from there, with other teachers of the time, moving on to adopt a permeation principle whereby we sought to infuse both the content and process dimensions of the curriculum with a multicultural constant. In practice, as Lynch and other writers have recognized,[67] this permeation approach called for a high degree of sensitivity and awareness, not to mention ingenuity and resourcefulness. For in order to ensure that the multicultural potential of everyday topic work, maths, science, stories, poetry and other curriculum foci was recognized and exploited we needed to be alert to opportunities, have access to appropriate resources and have created a classroom atmosphere where children felt able to discuss differences without embarrassment or hostility.

That this approach to the curriculum has found growing support among teachers is confirmed by the Little and Willey survey which found that 68 per cent of schools and 94 per cent of those with a concentration (30 per cent or more) of ethnic minority children had discussed the question.[68] Further endorsement for this approach, along with examples of how it might take on practical forms in different types of classrooms, is to be found in the report of the Schools Council project *Education for a Multiracial Society*.[69] The same project was also highly aware of the limitations of an approach that confined itself to curriculum review without an accompanying recognition of the prevalence of racism in the wider society, in the school itself through the hidden curriculum, and among teachers.[70] In voicing this caveat to any single-minded stress on curriculum change the report foreshadowed a broader perspective which has come to prominence of late. Known variously as 'anti-racist teaching'[71] and 'education for racial equality'[72] this aims to combine into a coherent educational philosophy principles of curriculum development and professional self-appraisal, as well as questions about discrimination and equality in schools and the wider society. Where it differs from the permeation tactic is in taking as its starting point an unequivocal opposition to racism, both among individuals and as part of a pervasive climate which is reinforced and perpetuated by the policies and practices of schools and other social institutions. We can find its echo in that section of the Swann report which urges educationists to 'identify and remove those practices and procedures which work . . . against people from any ethnic group, and to promote, through the curriculum, an appreciation and commitment to the principles of equality and justice on the part of all pupils'.[73]

Of course, it can be argued that very few teachers who advocate a culturally diverse curriculum would not also be opposed to racism and committed to equality. But unfortunately of late the debate has become so polarized that we often feel ourselves forced to decide between being a 'multiculturalist' or an 'anti-racist'.

We are led to believe that the two groups occupy irreconcilable camps of ideology and strategy, the multiculturalists advocating the celebration of diversity and the anti-racists placing their emphasis on the struggle for equality. In reality, however, the dichotomy appears as false and unnecessary, for when we look at the classroom practice of teachers we often find that the two approaches are mutually dependent, a point recognized by the School Curriculum Development Committee in its 'Agenda for Multicultural Teaching'.

> . . . in schools these are *not* polar opposites; they share a complex interrelationship. On the one hand, the celebration of diversity is no more than patronising tokenism unless it is accompanied by a fundamental belief in the equality of individuals from every background. On the other hand, equality of outcomes is unlikely to be attained unless the educational system is permeated with a real and fundamental sensitivity to diversity and a formal curriculum response. The 'multicultural' and 'anti-racist' approaches are therefore not *alternatives* but interlocking parts of one whole; each is essential, but neither is sufficient on its own.[74]

It is this idea of an interlocking relationship between the anti-racist and multicultural approaches which I have in mind when talking about anti-racist teaching and advocating that schools place the appreciation of cultural variation prominently on their agendas.

At class teacher level in the primary school it has a number of far-reaching implications: informing children about the facts of cultural and linguistic diversity in Britain today; working to pervade all aspects of the curriculum with a reflection of this diversity; helping children to accept differences of race, language and culture; encouraging discussion of racism and discrimination as they affect children and their families; appraising classroom practice to ensure that direct or indirect discrimination is not occurring. Important as such steps are, however, to be effective they would need an accompanying whole school commitment in the form of a policy statement.

We shall return to this question of school policy in Chapter 6, but for now let us summarize the main themes which this first chapter has examined.

Summary
In this chapter we have:
1. questioned the idea of Britain as a recently multiculturalized society by outlining the history of our cultural, linguistic and ethnic diversity;
2. drawn some parallels between responses to this diversity in the past and the present day position of minorities, their cultures and languages;
3. sketched a picture of the diversity of today's Britain, referring to some of the more important surveys and investigations;
4. discussed the pattern of responses at school level, drawing attention to the limitations of the four main approaches – 'treat them all the same', 'special needs', 'compensatory' and 'curriculum with multicultural aspects';
5. briefly examined the idea of 'anti-racist teaching' and the relationship between this and the 'celebration of diversity' approach with its emphasis on curriculum permeation;
6. concluded that the differences between these two perspectives need not be irreconcilable but, rather, should become mutually dependent;
7. signalled the need for a whole school response to accompany and support the efforts of individual practitioners.

Further reading
There are now several very readable publications which will help extend the picture given here of the historical dimension to Britain's diversity. In the language field, Price, G. (1984) *The Languages of Britain*, Edward Arnold is highly recommended. From a social history perspective, Holmes, C., ed., (1978) *Immigrants and Minorities in British Society*, Allen and Unwin, and Fryer, P. (1984) *Staying Power – the History of Black People in Britain*, Pluto, are well worth consulting. The most recent overview is to be found in Linguistic Minorities Project (1985) *The Other Languages of England*, Routledge and Kegan Paul. For a comprehensive review of different perspectives on multicultural education see Lynch, J. (1983) *The Multicultural Curriculum*, Batsford.

2 Children and diversity

In the previous chapter we set the scene for the discussion by charting the evolution of Britain's cultural diversity and reviewing the pattern of responses at school level. We now turn to the children who are themselves part of that diversity. Several themes need to be explored. What does diversity actually mean in the lives of children? One of the teachers whose work was mentioned earlier[1] suggested that sooner or later children became aware of the differences between themselves and others. How much evidence is there for a statement like this? If children do register differences what effects, if any, do they have on their perceptions of themselves and others? And why should this matter for the teacher? To begin with let us consider one particular child whose personal profile will help us to begin to answer some of these questions.

The child in question, Mariam, an 11-year-old of Muslim background, attends a Leicester primary school where the staff, as part of their involvement with the Schools Council Mother Tongue Project,[2] decided to carry out an investigation into the languages spoken by their pupils. When asked by her teacher 'Which languages do you speak?', Mariam replied:

> I speak English at school, Gujarati on my way home to my friends. I read books at Mosque in Urdu and I learn passages from the Koran in Arabic.

By way of an afterthought she added:

> My mum speaks Marathi.[3]

Mariam is not an unusual child. Regularly, now, teachers' conversations with children of other communities reveal a similarly complex interweaving of linguistic and cultural experiences which represents life for so many young people growing up in Britain. When combined with the findings of more systematic studies of diversity[4] carried out in different towns and cities the demographic picture constructed in the previous chapter is confirmed. But, as pointed out at the time, it is a picture that bears little resemblance to the monocultural, monolingual image that traditionally has been presented of Britain and that has formed one of the assumptions underpinning the curriculum of schools and the knowledge system that schools have sought to perpetuate.

Living with two cultures

The words of the 11-year-old remind us of some of the manifestations of today's diversity: not only that British citizens speak many languages and live many cultures, but that this diversity is remarkably durable. She refutes an assumption long held by teachers that, given time, minority cultures and languages will become little more than museum curiosities for communities who have long since become assimilated.

The child herself points to one of the reasons for the durability of her family's language and culture: she attends classes outside normal school hours in her local mosque, in her case to learn Urdu (in the case of other children throughout Britain to learn any one of the numerous languages that have long been actively promoted by the efforts of ethnic minority communities). Her mosque is part of a vast and growing network of community self-help schools operating, often on shoe-string budgets, in the twilight world after normal school hours. The scale of this undertaking is in itself an indication of the commitment of communities to sustain the use of community languages, as well as to develop historical and religious awareness among their young people. In Chapter 4 there will be an in-depth discussion of the work and role of community-run classes; here it is enough to note their importance in many children's lives.

The first point to make about these self-help groups is that they have existed for many years. The Linguistic Minorities Project revealed that the first Hebrew school in London was founded in 1904, and some Eastern European groups have been running classes for almost 40 years.[5] Despite this, as late as 1976, Verity Saifullah Khan[6] reported that many LEA officers and teachers either had no knowledge of such classes or did not acknowledge their significance in the general educational development of children. In terms of the numbers of children involved it would be difficult to arrive at reliable national figures but the Linguistic Minorities Project's 1981/2 surveys[7] of Bradford, Coventry and Haringey recorded almost 8,000 children attending classes regularly in those three areas alone.

That the classes occupy considerable importance for those families who support them is clear from the figures themselves. But why is so much importance attached to them? Mercer sheds some light on this:

> . . . it is when a minority are living among a powerful majority and feel the continuation of their own culture to be threatened that members of the

minority are likely to try self-consciously to keep ethnicity alive.[8]
She goes on:

> Concern exists that the language and traditions will disappear as the
> children are educated in the English language in state schools and exposed
> to Western influences through school, friends, television and so on.[9]

Community classes, then, are a 'product of dislocation'[10] and exist to
'bridge a gap' in the child's general education.[11]

It is sometimes argued that community-run classes hold essentially
conservative preservationist notions of what constitute their languages
and cultures: notions which derive in the main from older generations'
memories of life in the country of origin, and which are sometimes
overlaid with romanticized thoughts of eventual return. From this
position children tend to be seen as Cypriots, Italians or Pakistanis in
exile, and the function of the community schools becomes one of
stemming the tide of cultural and linguistic assimilation. In short, it is
argued that community classes are not accepting the changing
circumstances in which young people are growing up. Mercer puts it
this way:

> To gain status in the wider society some children may feel that they must
> abandon the traditional language and cultural practices and become more
> like members of the host community. Some of the organisers and teachers
> in the supplementary schools clearly see their task as being to counter such
> westernization.[12]

Although this may apply to some community schools others are
asserting the dual identity of their pupils as British Asians or British
Cypriots living, not in aspic, but in an urban multicultural society
which is giving rise to a re-interpretation of culture and new forms of
language evolving from the interchange taking place between their
own and others' experiences.

The idea of children and young people dynamically reinterpreting
the culture of their parents is a running theme for numerous writers
who themselves are from minority backgrounds. Maxine Hong
Kingston is a good example, having been born in California of Chinese
immigrant parents. She expresses it in this way:

> Those in the emigrant generations who could not assert brute survival died
> young and far from home. Those of us in the first American generation
> have had to figure out how the invisible world the emigrants built around
> our childhood fit in solid America.[13]

Later she addresses her community thus:

> Chinese-Americans, when do you try to understand what things in you are
> Chinese, how do you separate what is peculiar to childhood, to poverty,

insanities, one family, your mother who marked your growing up with stories, from what is Chinese? What is Chinese tradition and what is the movies?[14]

Similar questions are daily being asked by British-born minority group children and are being answered in a creative and eclectic way. Yet we still talk in negative terms about children being caught and torn between two cultures. Whilst I would not wish to disassociate myself totally from these arguments, especially when they pose searching questions related to the content of learning in schools,[15] we are increasingly finding, and the 11-year-old Mariam underscores the point, that although children often do live and alternate between two cultures the process is frequently more active and positive than was previously believed to be the case. Jane Miller advances a similar view:

> We have to recognise that people who grow up here, though they or their parents may have come from other places and ways of life, will not simply move between two cultures, comparing and contrasting, as it were, and making judicious selections from each. They will want to raid ours and reject a good deal of it, and they will be transforming the one they come from in the process. This will not be sad if it is understood, if what is lost and what is gained are properly valued.[16]

Elsewhere in her book Jane Miller talks about children being 'poised not stranded'[17] between their two cultural worlds. She sees their position as a mobile one in which they are well placed to make critical judgements about the two sides of the cultural divide and to deal positively with potential conflict between them. It is this relationship between tradition and 'the movies' which our 11-year-old and others like her are now in their own way trying to work out.

Children's linguistic repertoires

Mariam's statement above graphically reminds us of just how little teachers know about their pupils. She is not unusual in having developed the skills of alternating between, making selections from, and reworking where needed, the different cultures and languages that comprise her world. In addition she will almost certainly have a sharp sense of appropriateness, knowing when and where it is expected that she use a particular language, even a particular form of language. It is likely, for instance, that her English language repertoire will display a wide range of features, with the forms used, say, in the playground with friends being quite distinct from those used with the teacher in the classroom. At one level this means that bilingual children from quite an early age will often absorb the English dialect features – accent, vocabulary, idioms etc. – of the area where they live and that these will show up strongly in the daily round of playground, street and other situations where the peer group is paramount. Yet, at another level, when talking with the teacher, children will instinctively shift into the register of the classroom. To some degree the same could be expected of the Gujarati that the 11-year-old uses with peers and siblings in one setting, and parents and grandparents in another. Here, however, the picture beomes even more interesting if we apply the knowledge that we have gained from linguistic research related to the mixing of languages. We can turn, for instance, to the American linguist Weinreich[18] who talks about children and young people borrowing from their family language to use in their everyday English speech. This borrowing, he says, seems to occur 'in discourse that is informal and uninhibited by pretensions of high social status. Particularly apt to be transferred are colourful idiomatic expressions, difficult to translate, with strong affective overtones, whether endearing, pejorative or mildly obscene'.[19]

The notion of speakers moving between two (or more) languages or living in a language environment that comprises elements of both is akin to what linguists know as 'interlanguage'. Traditionally, teachers have regarded any mixing of languages, whether in terms of pronunciation, vocabulary or syntax, as errors to be eradicated. It is interesting however, to see that linguists[20] are currently describing this mixing as both an active learning process and a feature of cultural identity. In other words, bilinguals may use the blending of languages as a means of defining their ethnicity and forging a common sense of identity with others of the same ethnic group.[21] Jane Miller develops the idea further and links it in with our earlier theme of children having a varied language repertoire which they select from according to situation:

> It encourages a view of language users . . . as switching between codes or dialects or even languages in response to social as well as linguistic demands.[22]

For her it is part of a 'dialect continuum, which allows that most speakers will operate a language repertoire from, crudely, the more formal kind of language to the more intimate'.[23] As teachers we need to become more aware of this creative process in which so many of our pupils are engaged, not least because it will help us appreciate the depth of their experience and the sophistication of their skills.

Children's cultural repertoires
We can now develop the idea of a child having his or her own linguistic repertoire into thinking about a repertoire of cultural knowledge and capabilities. Here, too, our 11-year-old is helpful. We know from her language profile that she has access to a range of cultural contexts –

school, playground, street, Muslim home, mosque – which necessitate her using not only different languages but also different varieties of language. The picture goes further because, interwoven with her linguistic accomplishments, there is a proficiency in following different cultural rules and social roles: rules and roles relating to methods of addressing others, demonstrating deference or self-assertion and expressing friendship, gratitude and sadness, as well as the more visible manifestations of diversity – dressing, eating and worshipping. In short, this child, like so many others, leads a life comprising an intricate tapestry of cultural experiences, each with its own values, expectations, norms of behaviour and modes of communication.

Moreover, complex as this is, there is a further, often overlooked, cultural strand that needs to be mentioned. I am here alluding to the culture of childhood, the realm of songs, jokes, riddles and games which children create for themselves. We know from writers such as Sluckin[24] of the role which this plays in personal development as well as peer group relations. And we can turn to the Opies[25] for a fascinating tour of the realm itself with its regionally varied truce terms, chasing, catching and liberating procedures. its seasonally-based street and playground games, and its parodies on topical songs, stories and events. These are as integral to the daily activities of bilingual children as they are to others. Children newly arrived in Britain are soon initiated into them and, if born here, they grow up with them in the same way as we would expect indigenous[26] English children to do. In the multi-lingual school the whole process is further enriched through children drawing upon the childhood traditions of their family cultures. So it is not unusual in playgrounds to see and hear dipping rhymes, chasing games, counting and swapping rituals which, though originating in the overseas cultures of minority communities, are now firmly located in our multicultural society and thereby available to all.

It is this image of intermingling cultural worlds which I have in mind when talking about the 'tapestry' of children's experience. Sadly, though, they are worlds which for some teachers remain unfamiliar. Why is this? Without doubt much of the responsibility should rest squarely with schools themselves and the attitudes which some teachers continue to purvey, ranging from ignorance of, or disregard for, children's home cultures to, in some cases, open disapproval of their language preferences, eating habits and dress traditions. Amrit Wilson, writing about schools with a preponderance of Asian pupils, describes it in this way:

> Only a minority of teachers I spoke to were interested in the way of life of their Asian pupils and even a smaller number knew anything about it. This

lack of interest goes right through the education system . . . A girl of ten told me that children in her school were punished if they spoke in their own language. An Indian teacher said that in his school Asian children's names were almost invariably mispronounced. But when in one class he had taken the register and pronounced their names correctly, there had been some laughter from non-Indian children (who were a minority in the class) but floods of embarrassed giggles from Asian children, who seemed to prefer their names to be mispronounced in school.[27]

Amrit Wilson was writing in 1978 and although what she says will still hold true in some schools in parts of Britain nowadays, at the primary level at least, it is becoming more usual for teachers to display interest in the worlds which their pupils occupy outside school. Increasingly we find that primary teachers are turning to these worlds as potential sources of enrichment for the curriculum. Unfortunately teachers' interest is not always immediately rewarded and their sincerity is sometimes questioned. For children's sense of appropriateness about when to use their cultural and linguistic skills will often extend to include an adroitness at concealing those skills if they perceive them to be unwanted and unvalued. And this, despite the sincere intentions of individual teachers, can be their perception of the expectations of the school. Quite simply, if their skills are not known to be wanted they will be left, as Harold Rosen says, 'at the school gates'.[28]

Self-rejection and low self-esteem

Children's responses will take on a variety of forms. Sometimes these will involve public refusal to cooperate with the teacher's good intentions, a situation encountered by John Wright during his work with the Inner London Education Authority's Bilingual Education Project.[29] Wright describes how a Punjabi-speaking boy bridled at being asked by his teacher to use some Punjabi language materials, saying 'I don't need that. I can read English.'[30] The boy was offended by the teacher's well-intentioned efforts. Wright comments:

> We need to be sensitive about these kinds of responses, and try to understand them. Perhaps they are not surprising given that the languages . . . of Britain's minority groups are ignored and therefore, by implication, disparaged in many of our schools.[31]

In my own work teachers have reported numerous examples of how their genuine attempts to encourage intercultural and interlingual sharing have caused children to dissolve into giggles or lower their heads with embarrassment. Questions about the languages of home and community have revealed that children may sometimes deny speaking anything other than English. They may be unwilling or even unable to label their languages correctly, reporting that they speak

'Indian', 'Pakistani', or 'African' rather than Malayalam, Mirpuri Punjabi or Twi. This apparent self-rejection is not confined to language. Food, dress, worship and other aspects of family and community life have all proved similarly resistant to exploration in the classroom. To begin to understand why this has happened, and continues to happen, we need to enter the well-trodden field of research associated with 'self-concept' and 'self-esteem' among children. The reader wanting a detailed review of the subject can turn to a number of more specialized and easily accessible publications such as those by Davey[32] and Milner[33], or to writers such as Cohen and Manion[34] for a discussion of the research as it relates to the wider context of multicultural education. In the work that has been carried out, the dominant theme has been the self-image of the black child. From the early writings of Horowitz[35] and the Clarks[36] back in the 1930s and 1940s through the 1950s and 1960s with Mary Goodman[37] and into the last decade with Milner's highly influential studies[38] evidence has accumulated to suggest that black children[39] have identity problems as a result of being unable to come to terms with their ethnicity. Sometimes this might take the form of open self-rejection: in tests using doll choice techniques, photographs or interviews, black children time and again dismissed their own ethnicity and selected white subjects as being 'most like' themselves. In other cases, whilst having no difficulty identifying the subject who most resembled themselves, when asked to state their ethnic preference many again made a white 'out-group' choice. White children, on the other hand, had very few difficulties in providing the appropriate responses. Thus a succession of investigators were led to conclude that black children were frequently afflicted with a low self-image, and all the damaging consequences of such a condition, for mental health and educational achievement, were spelt out.

To say that these findings had an impact on education would be an understatement. Indeed, much of the rationale for multicultural education in the 1970s stemmed from them. Many of us will remember vividly how, newly alerted to the deleterious effects of black children's low self-esteem, we set about adjusting the curriculum and resources of our multicultural classrooms to reflect more overtly the cultural backgrounds of the children and thereby enhance their sense of self. In our most crusading moments we came to view ourselves as therapists charged with the responsibility of repairing the psychologically damaged. However, in the latter half of that decade and in the early 1980s, ideas were again changing. A different picture was emerging as researchers, now working in a climate of growing minority group 'consciousness' began to report a sharp decline in 'white-orientation'[40]

among black children and a much firmer self-understanding.[41] David
Milner explains it in this way:

> . . . black consciousness has grown, black social and political organisations
> have flourished and black culture has evolved a specifically 'British'
> variant, all of which has given black children and youth an alternative,
> acceptable image of their group with which to identify.[42]

Nurtured in this consciousness movement, and from the vantage point
of the 1980s, Maureen Stone[43] advances a radical critique of the
multicultural education movement's emphasis on raising the black
child's self-esteem. Calling upon her own research in black supplementary schools she argues, in essence, that black children do not have
the problem of low self-image that traditionally has been ascribed to
them. For her the low self-image theory is part of a 'pathological' view
of the black child which seeks to locate the causes of underachievement and low motivation in the psychological make up of the
individual. Thus, she argues, attention is distracted from the inherent
inequalities and injustices of the educational system. She goes on to
develop a searching attack on the 'affective-type goals' of multicultural
education and the teaching styles which accompany them, an argument which has provoked a strong reaction among several writers.[44]
We shall return to this theme later, but here let us consider what
Maureen Stone has to say about the 'pathological' view of the child, for
this is perhaps the most important aspect of her whole thesis. It needs
to be taken seriously because of its value in widening our perspective
beyond a single-minded preoccupation with the failings and deficiencies of the individual child to take in a more critical look at the
shortcomings of the educational system. In this way we are nearer to
understanding the difficulties reported earlier where teachers found
that their attempts to incorporate into the classroom elements of
children's cultural and linguistic experiences were thwarted by the
children's own resistance. If we accept the Stone argument, and I am
suggesting that we should, these difficulties come to be seen as
symptoms of a more deep-seated problem to do with the treatment of
the minority child's cultural being by both the school and the wider
society.

So for teachers wishing to take a more positive stance in relation to
classroom diversity the task facing them becomes a two-stranded
one. At a minimum level it calls for careful trust-building with children
in order to convey the message that difference of culture and language
are welcomed within the classroom. But these teachers need also to
acknowledge that celebration of diversity will not in itself be sufficient
– and indeed trust-building efforts can easily be negated – unless there

is an accompanying response to racism as it manifests itself in children's lives. The Swann report expresses it this way:

> . . . it is difficult for ethnic minority communities to have full confidence and trust in an institution which they see as simply ignoring or dismissing what is in fact an ever present and all-pervasive shadow over their everyday lives.[45]

From the discussion so far the reader might be forgiven for concluding that our interest here is solely with ethnic minority children. Nothing could be further from the truth. The white, so called indigenous, children should also feature prominently in the argument being constructed, not least because the quality of pupil-to-pupil relationships is crucial to our understanding of how schools can either devalue or validate the diversity that children bring with them. Also, it should not be forgotten that diversity of culture and language is not restricted to those children whose families have their origins overseas.

Race awareness in children

Traditionally, teachers have maintained that children in the early years of the primary school are not themselves aware of differences. They play together quite happily, the argument runs, without any regard for skin colour or cultural variation. It is only as they get older and come under the influence of the outside world that race becomes a factor in their relationships with others.[46] Comforting as it may be, however, this 'colour blind' image of children bears little resemblance to reality. Over 30 years ago the American researcher Mary Goodman, using evidence from a study of four-year-olds, concluded that:

> . . . little children sometimes pay a startling amount of attention to race . . . they are ready to pay attention to race just as soon as they pay attention to other physical and socially significant attributes like age and sex.[47]

Marsh, one of the earlier British writers in the field, reached similar conclusions. Also working with a group of nursery age children, he found that . . . 'the degree of knowledge of racial differences exhibited by the very young . . . was often remarkable'.[48] He described a developmental phase of 'racial curiosity' during which children frequently ask about differences of skin colour and hair texture, the 'critical age' for which seemed to fall between about three and three-and-a-half years. This notion of developmental growth in children's racial awareness was explored by Mary Goodman in a later edition of the book already mentioned.[49] There she sets out a process of three overlapping stages through which children's attitudes on race seem to progress. The first, akin to Marsh's 'racial curiosity', is a straightforward perceptual 'awareness' of racial differences. The second, 'racial orientation', marks the beginning of feelings and evaluative responses towards people of different racial groups. The third and final stage represents the formation of attitudes as we know them.

Though subsequently criticized by other writers[50] Goodman's schema does offer us a basis for looking fairly systematically at what happens to children's attitudes as they develop. We can now add detail to it by briefly reviewing some of the other major pieces of research in the field. Several studies[51] set the age of the onset of race awareness, that is, the ability to recognize the differences of race and categorize people accordingly, at anywhere between two and five years. For instance, Morland,[52] one of the principal contributors, has suggested that this ability is well-established by the age of three and improves steadily up to the age of six. Of course, it can always be argued that the awareness of racial differences is a natural phase in children's cognitive and perceptual development and need not, in itself, give any cause for concern. Indeed, similar observations might be made about the evidence which suggests that from an equally early age children will often show a preference for members of their own racial group and a desire to mix and play with them rather than with others. True, 'in-group' preferences do not necessarily indicate antipathy towards people of other skin colours but, as Kenneth Clark, one of the more significant researchers in the field, has argued, they do imply that some form of evaluation is taking place on a racial basis:

> The child's first awareness of racial differences is . . . associated with some rudimentary evaluation of these differences . . . the child cannot learn what racial group he belongs to without being involved in a larger pattern of emotions, conflicts and desires which are part of his growing knowledge of what society thinks about his race.[53]

Although in the very early years of perceptual development this evaluation may be at an unconscious level, children soon begin to articulate their feelings in any one of several ways. David Milner comments, for example, on the spontaneous remarks about black figures which children have voiced during the course of attitude tests: 'He's a stinky little boy, take him away.', 'I don't like him he's a blackie.', 'He's no good.', 'He kills people.'[54] Referring to one of the major American studies, he describes how simple evaluative remarks may later give way to crude stereotypes:

> Among the reactions to the black dolls in this study were the following: 'He's coming out of jail.', 'They are gangsters.', 'He would be digging dirt.', 'He doesn't have no work.', 'He's a coloured and he carries knives.'.[55]

and how children seem to have no difficulty acquiring an understanding of the way society views the social worth of black people:

> An indication of this was the children's allocation of poor housing and menial employment to black people (and superior environments to whites) in doll and picture tests.[56]

It is this tendency to register, internalize and reiterate the prevailing messages about black people which seems to characterize Goodman's third phase, as children from the age of about seven and up to early adolescence display 'a gradual intensification of prejudice'.[57]

At this stage it would be prudent to note that much of the evidence so far quoted has been compiled from work carried out with children in experimental situations. We therefore need to know of the degree to which these same observations show themselves in children's day-to-day activities. Is there necessarily any similarity between experimental evidence and the way children actually behave? As one might expect there is no clear cut answer to this but to gain some purchase on it we can turn initially to some of the sociometric studies of friendship preferences among primary age children. Working in the late 1960s Rowley[58] and Kawwa[59] undertook studies of friendship choices with samples that included primary age children. Both revealed a strong tendency for children to select friends from their own ethnic groups. A few years later Durojaiye[60] confirmed the pattern in a study of junior age pupils. Here, too, ethnicity was an important factor in the choice of friends but, significantly, the white children in the sample adhered to own-group choices far more closely than did the black minority children. Possibly the largest study so far has been that conducted by Jelinek and Brittan.[61] Using a national sample of over 4,000 children at the ages 8, 10, 12 and 14 they, too, found that race was a major consideration for children as they went about selecting friends. Furthermore, there was no appreciable difference in this respect between their eight-year-olds and their 14-year-olds.

Racist attitudes

For real life evidence of how children's, especially white children's, own-group preferences in friendship will often be accompanied by evaluations of other cultures and ethnic groups we can turn once again to the Swann Report. Particularly informative are the Annexes in which Arnold Matthews and Laurie Fallows report on their visits to schools 'with few or no ethnic minority pupils'. Consider this case study by Arnold Matthews:[62]

LEA B
1. In many ways the attitudes I encountered during my visits to schools in

LEA B were similar to those encountered in LEA A. The same insularity of outlook was reflected in the schools; teachers were equally preoccupied with their curricula and little attention was paid to the need to prepare pupils for life in a multi-racial society. Indeed, the major difference was that there tended to be a rather more visible ethnic minority presence both within school and in the surrounding area and thus a more readily identifiable 'target' for racist attitudes.

School B1

1. This large infants school was an example of the resourceful, adaptable school in an area of growing population. The headteacher was supported wholeheartedly by a deeply caring and conscientious staff. In keeping with the general picture of great care and attention being devoted to the needs of all pupils there was evidence of the few ethnic minority children being given a warm welcome and favourable provision.

2. The Head emphasised that the hidden curriculum fosters positive attitudes of tolerance and goodwill amongst all kinds and groups of people including the application of the Good Samaritan story to a foreigner 'without having to underline it'. The teaching staff included a former white African who had accepted the 'racial divide' without question but is now totally converted in her attitudes towards black people and expressed positive ideas about multicultural education. Teacher after teacher confidently expressed the conviction that no racial prejudice had been found from parents or children.

3. Arrangements were made for a group of about ten of the most articulate older children to join me in the Head's room during the afternoon. They were confident and talkative and the conversation flitted briefly from topic to topic. Suddenly one child described a holiday spent in Wales where she had seen some black children peeping at her out of a caravan. Asked whether she talked or played with them she answered, 'Oh no. I didn't want to play with black children'. Another little girl then blurted out 'I don't like black people, only Sarah' (one of the group present). Other children spontaneously chimed in 'Nor I'. I narrated this incident to the Head afterwards and she was deeply shocked by the revelation. The Deputy Head, however admitted that she had had a similar experience with children in her class some months before. She had not however reported it to the Head.

Sadly, it is not an isolated example either among the numerous case studies presented by the report or the anecdotal accounts that one frequently receives from teachers who have consciously stepped out of the 'colour-blind' ethos of their schools and sought to uncover for themselves what children are actually thinking.

For many children the dress, eating habits and hairstyles of ethnic minorities are all legitimate subjects for ridicule, jokes and taunts, as is skin colour. The pervasiveness of this abuse, this 'particular manifestation of racism within schools' is well-documented by Swann and was an issue on which the committee received 'a considerable amount of evidence'.[63] Notice how the report quite unequivocally chose to see it as a 'manifestation of racism' – a very significant move which consciously breaks with the traditional approach of denying the existence of racism among children, or at least playing it down on the grounds that children have always been given to name-calling and inter-personal taunts:

> Some teachers have argued that this (racist name-calling) is no different from the normal name-calling in which even young children may indulge and which is entirely harmless both in intent and long-term effect.[64]

For some teachers, then, calling another child 'nig-nog', 'paki', or whatever other term is current, is qualitatively no different from ridiculing some other aspect of the person – 'fatty', 'spotty', etc. The report reacts in this way:

> We believe the essential difference between racist name-calling and other forms of name-calling is that whereas the latter may be related only to the individual characteristics of a child, the former is a reference not only to the child but also by extension to their family and indeed more broadly their ethnic community as a whole. Racist name-calling, and its frequent companion racist grafitti, can thus convey to a child the accepted value judgement which the majority community has passed on his or her group and . . . where this value judgement is internalised by an individual and in time by a community this can only serve to strengthen and perpetuate the overall climate of racism in which they find themselves.[65]

To this we should add that such forms of abuse are equally damaging for the child who voices them since they are indicative of the degree to which she or he has been affected by the prevailing norms of behaviour and has, thereby, also become a victim of racism.

Cultural and linguistic prejudices

I would like to conclude this chapter in the way it began with a discursive example drawn from one child's experience, or rather in this case an adult's recollection of a childhood event:

> My own early political memories include being stood up, at eight years old, in front of my classmates in a Scottish primary school until I could correct the mistake I'd made reading aloud. I couldn't see the mistake. After an hour the teacher revealed that my heinous error had been to pronounce the word 'poor' as it is spelt rather than as 'pore'. That taught me several lessons. One was that the language my family spoke at home – the agricultural northeast of Scotland – was wrong. Not good enough. I looked at them with different eyes after that. It also taught me that my teacher,

with the best of intentions for my future, wanted me to speak 'properly', the English way.[66]

Unlike the child who was so helpful earlier in furnishing us with insights into the dimensions of diversity this one is not a member of one of the conventional ethnic minority groups. Instead he belongs to 'Britain's largest national minority',[67] the Scots, and as such serves to remind us that the issues with which we are concerned are not to be found solely in schools where there are substantial numbers of black children. Indeed, his description of that classroom encounter and the lessons learnt from it might well strike a chord for others who spent their early lives in communities where the English spoken was not of the sort normally promoted by schools.

Notions of correct and proper English run deep in our education system and teachers have frequently felt themselves to be responsible for their defence and preservation. To be fair, however, teachers have not been alone in holding such firm views about the social worth of different speech forms. Through the work of writers such as Giles and Powesland[68] we know that among the population at large speakers of Southern Standard English are usually assigned higher social status and believed to be more able and intelligent people; by contrast, speakers of regional dialects are often regarded as ignorant, un-educated and lacking in social finesse. Widespread as this belief is, however, there is no doubt that the education system should take much responsibility for perpetuating the situation. In a valuable review of how dialect has fared in schools over the years, Viv Edwards[69] draws attention to some of the officially received viewpoints. For instance, the Newbolt Report (1921) on *The Teaching of English in England* mentioned that:

> It is emphatically the business of the Elementary School to teach all its pupils who speak a definite dialect or whose speech is disfigured by vulgarisms, to speak standard English, and to speak it clearly, and with expression.[70]

Similar sentiments were echoed in the Spens Report (1939) on Secondary Education which referred to the 'slovenly, ungrammatical and often incomprehensible' nature of the 'English in common usage'.[71] Later publications, for example the Newsom Report of 1963, went on to discuss the relationship between language usage and educational achievement, attributing much of the failure of working class children to the deficiencies of their language.

The deficit philosophy

For Edwards, a 'particularly influential' figure in the whole debate was

Basil Bernstein whose theories of elaborated and restricted codes,[72] she argues, provided 'a veneer of academic respectability to prejudices about the inadequacy of non-Standard English and the linguistic shortcomings of dialect speakers'.[73]

Many of us know only too well from our own experience how Bernstein's theories were soon seized upon by teachers, absorbed into the lexicon of staffroom discussion, and became a convenient ever-present explanation for the difficulties which working class children met in the classroom. We had to wait until the late 1960s and early 1970s for any substantial countervailing arguments. These came from a variety of sources. Teachers themselves, at an intuitive level, were becoming concerned about the deleterious effect which the 'deficit' view might have on children's self-perceptions and, thereby, their motivation to learn. At the same time some teachers were beginning to question the appropriateness of the traditional curriculum for working class children. Their ideas were crystallized by Eric Midwinter and others associated with the early 1970s Educational Priority Area (EPA) movement. Essentially, Midwinter's argument was one of cultural relativism which maintained that working class children were rejecting school and, by implication, any chances of educational success because of a curriculum which was irrelevant to them and their cultural worlds. For Midwinter, schools were failing 'to relate to the experiences of their pupils and their catchment area'; the curriculum was 'irrelevant to the community, its children and both their needs.'[74]

The American linguist, William Labov, focused his criticisms on the notion of linguistic deprivation. Analysing the grammar of American Black English he demonstrated that, rather than being a substandard and 'broken' version of standard English, this had its own distinct logic, grammatical coherence and rule system – and furthermore displayed a flexibility and sophistication of use which standard English itself often lacked.[75] English writers such as Harold Rosen[76] and Susan Houston[77] advanced similar arguments in relation to white working class children in Britain.

A major impetus and a timely official seal of approval for the anti-deficit movement came in the form of the Bullock report's now famous proposition that:

> No child should be expected to cast off the language and culture of the home as he crosses the school threshold nor to live and act as though school and home represent two totally separate and different cultures.[78]

Compared to the 1960s and early 1970s there is now, without doubt, a far more welcoming and open-minded attitude among teachers towards pupils' ways of living and communicating. But I am never quite sure of the extent to which this essentially philosophical position has been translated into classroom practice and adopted as a guiding principle in all aspects of teachers' dealings with their pupils. Certainly there are many teachers who are consciously enacting the ideals they embrace – but what about the others?

Discontinuity in thinking

In terms of language policies, at least, I suspect there may be some discontinuity between theoretical ideals and day-to-day practice. The sentiment of parity of esteem between the classroom's varied linguistic forms may be 'uttered much more than it is understood and very very much more often than it is implemented.'[79] In these circumstances we would be advised to remind ourselves of what some of the prominent writers in the field have to say about the importance of a classroom approach that values the different linguistic varieties that children are able to bring with them.

In the teaching of reading, we know from the work of Goodman and Buck[80] that dialect speakers will often 'appropriate' a text. In other words, they may translate a standard English passage into the variety of English with which they feel most comfortable. Rather than being errors, these dialect-based deviations, or 'miscues' as Goodman calls them, show that the child is actively engaging with the passage and is having little difficulty extracting meaning from it. Yet teachers' instinctive reaction is often to intervene and either request that the 'correct' standard form be given or, if it is not forthcoming, to supply it themselves. Berdan, writing about speakers of Black English – but there is no reason to assume that his observations are applicable only to them – puts it as follows:

> The teacher's attention focuses primarily on the form of what is being read. All too often successful reading is assumed to mean the use of Standard English pronunciation and grammar. This assumption is often expressed by the demand that children 'read what they see'. The result is that a child's oral reading is often interrupted by a demand for a Standard English equivalency for some Black English word used.[81]

For some children the teacher's interventions come fast and frequent and can have the most disastrous consequences:

> Many children find that they must submit to these episodes every time they read aloud . . . Their effect on the continuity of reading instruction is deadening. Children learn to cope by reading slower so that they will encounter fewer possible interruptions, by reading at a barely audible level so that teachers cannot determine exactly what was said, or by simply refusing to read at all.[82]

A similar process of teacher intervention often occurs during talk activities in the classroom. Again we can turn to Berdan for illustration:

> . . . when a Black English speaking child inquires, 'What do this word mean?' the teacher may respond by saying, 'What does that word mean? Now ask your question again.'[83]

Berdan is quick to point out that the teacher's action may be well-intentioned:

> Usually it seems that the intent of the teachers is to provide the child with a Standard English model and to encourage its use in the classroom.[84]

But the child is likely to place an alternative interpretation on it:

> . . . withdraw from active participation in the classroom, and in particular avoid any speaking that might draw criticism, implicit or explicit.[85]

This simple survival strategy is one that children learn very quickly and sometimes with disastrous consequences, for it can cause enthusiasm to be lost and a negative impression to be transmitted of the child's desire to learn.

Dialect features in children's writing probably evoke the strongest feelings among teachers, and not surprisingly it is probably in this area that we find most inconsistency in thinking:

> Some schools, for example, may accept and even encourage the use of dialect in speech (role play, drama etc.) but have a school language policy which urges the use of standard English in writing. It is not unknown for schools to state that they will not display writing in dialect on the classroom walls.[86]

There seem to be a number of common characteristics in the ways in which teachers often respond to children's dialect features as they appear in writing. First, there is a tendency to assume that writing in dialect must, per se, be inferior in quality to that which is based more firmly on standard English. In other words, we see at work the same equation that classifies the speakers of non-standard forms as being intellectually and socially inferior to others. Yet there seems to be some evidence that dialect users have a 'sensitivity to situation'[87] which leads them to make far less use of dialect features when writing than when engaged in spoken activities. Second, it is not unusual for dialect features, for instance, different rules relating to subject-verb agreement, use of the article or the preposition, to be confused with straightforward technical difficulties and for the work to be penalized accordingly. Here, too, close analysis of children's writing can be helpful since it frequently shows that technical errors are a far more prevalent and a more serious barrier to understanding then the presence of dialect.[88]

The net outcome of all this is a very unsatisfactory state of affairs where teachers feel compelled to 'correct', often at the expense of paying attention to content; whilst, in some cases, knowing that to 'correct' everything would be both impracticable for the marker and disheartening for the child. What is called for, then, if we are to avoid the anomalies we have described, is a sensitive handling of the child's own language forms. Referring to it as the Repertoire Approach, the Swann report describes it in this way:

> (this approach) values all languages and dialects as an important part of the child's linguistic repertoire. The intention is not to change or replace any particular dialect but to develop a sharper awareness of, and interest in, the different language forms that the child can use, thus avoiding confusion between them . . . the 'repertoire' approach focusses on what the child can do and builds constructively on the considerable linguistic strengths the child brings to the classroom.[89]

Above all, as Viv Edwards stresses, we need to appreciate the role that dialect plays in the child's life and cultural being:

> Much of the retention of dialect features in both speech and writing can almost certainly be explained in terms of the very close relationship between language and identity. The teacher who constantly criticises and 'corrects' may well be perceived as rejecting the dialect speaker's culture and values. And it is important to remember that the child's own community, in particular the peer group, exercises far more powerful control over the child's language than the teacher.[90]

Although the main concern in this chapter has been with cultural diversity as it affects children, it has been interesting to note the number of occasions when attention has turned to teachers. This is hardly surprising in view of the part which teachers play in the development of children's cultural awareness. In effect there has been a sub-theme to the chapter and it is this which is now picked up in Chapter 3 where teachers and cultural diversity are considered.

Summary

In this chapter we have:
1. identified some of the dimensions of cultural and linguistic variation among children;
2. drawn attention to the creative ways in which children may reconcile potential conflict between cultures;
3. called into question the notion of 'low self-image' among ethnic minority children;

4. highlighted some of the factors which influence how children perceive their own cultures and those of others;
5. discussed the growth and manifestation of racial feelings among children;
6. stressed some of the similarities between the treatment of black ethnic minority cultures and the cultures of children from 'indigenous' minorities and working class communities.
7. made reference to the influence which teachers can have on the development of children's awareness of their own and each other's cultures.

Further reading
The work of community-run classes is given fuller treatment in Linguistic Minorities Project (1985) *The Other Languages of England*, Routledge and Kegan Paul. Their role in maintaining a sense of ethnicity among young people is touched upon in Mercer, L. (1981) 'Ethnicity and the Supplementary School', in Mercer, N. (1981), ed., *Language in School and Community*, Edward Arnold. A book which brings alive, through personal experience, many of the themes of this chapter is Hong Kingston, M. (1981) *The Woman Warrior*, Picador. The most comprehensive examination of research relating to race awareness and ethnic identity in children is Milner, D. (1983) *Children and Race, Ten Years On*, Ward Lock. More detailed examination of language issues, with a strong classroom emphasis, is to be found in Edwards, V. (1983) *Language in Multicultural Classrooms*, Batsford, and the Open University Pack, *Every Child's Language*, Multilingual Matters.

3 Teachers and diversity

Teachers stand at the point of delivery between the education service and the individual child. The effectiveness with which the service is delivered will be crucially affected by teachers, their commitment, knowledge and skills and, above all, their attitudes. It is thus appropriate that, having spent the previous chapter discussing how cultural diversity will present itself in the lives of children, attention should now be turned to teachers. There is much to discuss here. For multicultural schools, teachers' expectations of, and attitudes towards, ethnic minority pupils are issues which must be addressed. For all schools, teachers' responses to cultural forms other than their own, as well as their views about the very notion of education for cultural diversity, are themes to be explored further. Coverage of these subjects will form the early part of this chapter. During the course of it we will highlight shortcomings in how teachers think and behave, but it is important that such criticisms should lead on to constructive proposals for action. The final sections of the chapter will therefore be devoted to questions of professional development.

Teachers' expectations

There can be few teachers who have not come across Rosenthal and Jacobson's classic 1968 study, *Pygmalion in the Classroom*.[1] This work, more than any other, brought the attention of the educational world to the effect of teachers' expectations on children's classroom performance. For the first time on any significant scale, we had an experiment which showed that, in the authors' own words:

> When teachers expected that certain children would show greater intellectual development, those children did show greater intellectual development.

It is hardly surprising that the findings generated a great deal of controversy among teachers and no shortage of criticism from other researchers.[2] In subsequent years further studies produced similar results, whilst also shedding light on how teachers' expectations are likely to influence their actions within the classroom. Rist[3] found that after only a few days in a kindergarten class children were assigned by their teacher to one of three tables in accordance with the teacher's assessment of their ability – 'bright', 'average', or 'below average'. The teacher's judgement had been formed on the basis of superficial information about the children's social and economic circumstances. As a result the three tables came to represent three distinct social class strata: the cleaner, more affluent children on Table 1 and the unkempt, poorer children on Table 3. Needless to say, the black members of the class tended to gravitate towards the 'bottom' table. Once placed at their tables, the children found themselves receiving differential treatment from the teacher. Table 1 children were called upon more often to answer questions and recount experiences. Physically they were nearer to the teacher and so came in for more of her attention. Consequently they were much more attuned to what was going on generally in the classroom. IQ measures at the end of the kindergarten year showed no significant differences among the children, yet the ability groupings were reinforced in the next year's First Grade class. By the time Rist observed the children in the Second Grade, Table 3 had taken on many of the characteristics of a slow learner's group; disruptive behaviour was well-established and, predictably, the teacher's relationship with her pupils was more controlling than supportive.

The race dimension was examined more specifically by Rubovitz and Maehr[4] in a study which involved observing teachers who had been informed that certain children in their classes were 'gifted' and others 'non-gifted'. The results were quite alarming. The 'gifted', white children received a disproportionate amount of the teachers' attention. Not only were they praised and encouraged more but their teachers, when interviewed, also described them as the brightest and most popular members of the class. By contrast, the black children were on the receiving end of the most negative treatment from their teachers, but it was the 'gifted' blacks for whom the harshest handling seemed to be reserved. It was almost as if the teachers held a stereotype of black children as disruptive and low-achieving and were resentful towards those who did not conform with this.

In a further study[5] Rosenthal described four distinct ways in which teachers' expectations can operate in the classroom and influence children's performance. He referred to these as 'climate', 'feedback', 'input' and 'output'. It might be helpful to expand on these features as they are likely to provide food for thought for teachers who wish to monitor their own classroom behaviour. Facial expressions, tone of voice and body language can all create a 'climate' which is just as effective as words in conveying positive or negative feelings towards children. 'Feedback' in the form of acknowledgement and praise is vital to children's progress and performance in the classroom. As we have seen, however, this is often distributed unevenly. 'Good' and 'gifted' pupils, by comparison with others, are rarely ignored when they volunteer answers to questions. And they are praised far more for the answers they give. Higher expectations are likely to lead the teacher to giving more 'input', in the form of direct teaching and more demanding material, to 'gifted' children. These pupils also have greater opportunity for 'output': they are asked more and harder questions, they are given more time for their responses and more prompting towards correct answers.

The picture that now emerges is a disturbing one, made all the more so by the evidence that teachers continue to hold negative stereotypes, especially of children of West Indian origin.[6] Caution is called for, however, when it comes to arguing that there is a causal relationship between teachers' attitudes and expectations and the underachievement of ethnic minority pupils. A number of writers, of whom Short[7] is one of the most recent, have warned against such a simplistic equation. For, as the Swann Report[8] stresses, the interplay between attitudes, expectations and achievement is a subtle and complex one. Even so, the fact remains that some ethnic minority children find themselves in situations where teachers' negative stereotypes and low expectations combine with an inappropriate curriculum and an unsupportive school ethos; and although it may be difficult to demonstrate empirically the full effect of this combination on children's learning we can be sure that it will do little to create a positive classroom environment.

Teachers' attitudes to multicultural education

Teachers' views about the role of education in preparing children for living with cultural diversity have been the focus of several studies since the early 1970s. One of the most comprehensive was Elaine Brittan's survey[9] of over 500 teachers in 25 primary and secondary schools, where the proportions of ethnic minority children ranged between 18 and 24 per cent. The results showed strong support (94 per cent) for the principle that 'schools have a responsibility to promote good race relations among pupils'. Over 75 per cent agreed that RE and Assemblies should reflect the faiths of minority groups. There was positive support, too, (67 per cent) for the suggestion that school syllabuses should be revised to include some coverage of the culture and countries of origin of ethnic minority children. However, the teachers were much less supportive of the proposition that 'schools should adapt their ways' to accommodate pupils' different cultural traditions. Here, less than 50 per cent were in favour of the suggestion and over 33 per cent disagreed or strongly disagreed. Clues to the discrepancy between this and the earlier responses were to be found in the teachers' accompanying comments. Some felt that adaptation should only happen when there are significant numbers of children in the school from other cultures; others were afraid of an adverse effect on the indigenous children. Many took a strongly assimilationist line:

> I think it is far better for immigrant children to merge in with the English pupils and not to keep on emphasising their differences . . . Far too much emphasis is given to the theory that English people should modify their way of life to suit the immigrant.

How is it, then, that teachers could, on the one hand, be in favour of reflecting cultural differences in certain curriculum areas whilst, on the other, not see any need for a broader review of policy and practice? Brittan explains the anomaly in two ways. For some teachers, she argues, it is not so much a question of being resistant to the school taking greater account of cultural variation but rather of being unsure of how to set about doing this. With other teachers she is less charitable:

> . . . the implication might be drawn that when faced with a suggestion that something rather more fundamental than merely imparting information about the religions and homelands of minority groups is required then there is considerably greater reluctance to change, notably, if this might affect the ethos of the school or be seen as a threat to its traditional cultural identity.

In other words, superficial modification of the curriculum can be accomplished with a minimum of disruption to school policy and established methods of working. But resistance is more likely to arise when the changes being proposed involve more than minor adjustment to the content of Assemblies and RE and call instead for a reappraisal of the full curriculum as well as the values and assumptions under-pinning it. Whilst much of this resistance could be attributed to teachers' traditonal conservatism and reluctance to change, Brittan also points to a more fundamental explanation:

> That many teachers believe assimilation (although they often use the term 'integration' to describe this philosophy) to be the aim of our multicultural society, seems unquestionable.

The next substantial investigation came a few years later with Little and Willey's Schools Council Project *Studies in the Multi-ethnic Curriculum.*[10] Admittedly their purpose was more to survey what had been achieved by schools and LEAs in terms of multicultural education than to assess the attitudes of teachers. Nevertheless, in collating responses from teachers in a wide range of schools, the project was able to offer a comprehensive review of developments on the attitudinal front. The findings suggested that, in multicultural schools at least, a more encouraging picture was emerging. There was generally more enthusiasm about the need for more pervasive curriculum change and there was some evidence of school-based INSET to bring this about. However, some 15 per cent of schools with 'medium' or 'high' concentrations of ethnic minority children were still preoccupied with the need for integration and there was widespread fear that emphasizing differences would have a divisive effect on relationships among pupils. Typical of the responses was this one:

> I feel this whole area is being inflated to assume unreasonable proportions. This treatment will perpetuate the problem it seeks to cure. The aim must be to integrate, not differentiate.

Attitudinal barriers to progress were mentioned repeatedly in the replies from LEAs:

> We need to help teachers develop positive attitudes towards cultures other than their own . . .

> The major difficulty is intransigent attitudes, from unawareness to outright prejudice.

These observations were confirmed by the 300 replies received from predominantly white schools, over 90 per cent of which saw no need to modify their aims and practices in order to reflect present day diversity. Replies like the following were not unusual:

> Given the overall preponderance of white British children in the school such modification has not been found necessary.

When asked about teachers' in-service training needs for multicultural education, over 60 per cent of the schools saw the issue as unimportant, irrelevant or of low priority:

> There are so many other important topics for in-service training that I would put a course on the implications of a multi-ethnic society very low on my list.

So the findings of the survey showed that despite more encouraging signs among teachers in multicultural schools, the prevailing attitudes among colleagues in predominantly white classrooms were becoming a source of considerable concern. The situation seemed to have changed little by the time the Swann Committee made its report. Indeed the committee chose to devote much of its attention to the issue. The approach was to commission two experienced LEA Advisers, Arnold

Matthews and Laurie Fallows, to 'undertake case studies of the views and practices found within a number of "all-white" schools'.[11] In total, the two visited 26 schools, both primary and secondary, in six LEAs. Their reports, included as Annexes[12] to the main Swann Report represent the most recent large-scale surveys available. That the Swann Committee endorsed their findings is clear:

> In our view these reports provide a valuable insight into the attitudes and behaviour found in 'all-white' areas and schools in relation to ethnic minorities and illustrate vividly the gap which exists between the pronouncements and exhortations made at national level about the need to educate all pupils for life in a multi-racial society, and the extent to which such an aim is accepted and acted upon.[13]

The reports are full in their coverage and have much to say about the curriculum of the schools, evidence of racism among pupils and the factors influencing pupils' attitudes. And, of particular relevance to our present discussion, the two writers also make observations about the teachers they met.

With the exception of 'a few committed multiculturalists' the majority of the teachers were found to be 'preoccupied with the immediate concerns of their day-to-day teaching activities and believed that "multicultural" considerations were irrelevant both to them and to their pupils'.[14] Some, of course, showed greater awareness than others of the need for a multicultural dimension in the curriculum but overall there was little evidence that awareness had been translated into classroom actuality. As far as the teachers' attitudes were concerned, these displayed: 'the whole gamut of racial misunderstandings and folk mythology . . . racial stereotypes were common and attitudes ranged from the unveiled hostility of a few, through the apathy of many and the condescension of others, to total acceptance by a minority'.[15] Repeatedly, fears were expressed that any move to take account of diversity would generate controversy among staff and parents and cause unnecessary strife and division among pupils. Anxieties were especially strong on questions of racism. The teachers were not totally oblivious to racist incidents, jokes and abuse among children but few were convinced that intervention on their part would do anything but exacerbate the situation. Yet, in spite of the mood of despondency which prevails throughout the main Report's discussion of the 'All-White Schools Project', a positive note is sounded:

> . . . it was . . . encouraging to find that in a number of schools, the teachers professed themselves ready and willing to reappraise their own work and prepared to consider the need for a broader approach to their pupils' learning.[16]

Similar statements emerged from discussions with most of the LEAs. But, for this reappraisal to happen, it was felt strongly that teachers should receive more guidance and support than had hitherto been available to them.

Of course a 'committed multiculturalist' might argue, with some justification, that there is already a considerable amount of guidance and support available to teachers in the form of publications, classroom resources and INSET materials, and all that is lacking is a clear indication of will on the teachers' part. Even so we would probably all acknowledge that there have been few attempts to set out in any detail just what teachers require in the form of professional competence if they are to meet the challenge of cultural diversity.

Teachers and diversity – an action programme

In order to help draw together the several themes which have emerged so far into a coherent action programme, the remainder of this chapter will be used to offer a framework for the main areas of knowledge and interpersonal and professional skills which teachers need to be developing. The discussion which follows draws on the work of the American teacher/educator Geneva Gay.[17] By way of preface it needs to be stressed that what is here proposed is not intended as a complete prototype for the development of teachers. That would be beyond the scope of this particular book. Rather, it is designed as a self-monitoring guide for use by teachers who wish to have an overview of their own professional growth. The following chart summarizes the main components of the framework:

Responding to diversity:
knowledge and skills needed by teachers

Conceptual awareness
1. Understanding the main concepts of multicultural education and the implications of these for the classroom.
2. Understanding the historical background to multicultural education and how the concept has evolved.
3. Becoming familiar with the 'founders' and 'framers' of multicultural education.

Ethnic literacy
1. Understanding the way of life of different ethnic groups.
2. Learning how to process information about different cultures and lifestyles.
3. Understanding the presence and influence of ethnic minority groups in the shaping of British history, life and culture.

Professional applications
1. Translating knowledge about multicultural education and cultural diversity into classroom practice.
2. Acquiring the ability to analyse and clarify one's own values, attitudes, expectations and behaviour towards ethnically different groups and individuals.
3. Developing appropriate teaching styles and professional methods of working.
4. Knowing how to evaluate the school climate, curriculum and resources.

Let us now consider each of these areas in turn, with some examples of what they might mean in practice.

Conceptual awareness
It is here suggested that teachers should be familiar with the characteristics of cultural and ethnic diversity in Britain, as well as the fundamental concepts of multicultural education, its development over the years, the different interpretations of it and how these relate to each other and to classroom actuality. In addition, teachers need to know about the human and material resources which are available. We might call this an 'initial orientation stage'.

1. *Understanding the main concepts of multicultural education and the implications of these for the classroom*
The main point to be made here is that multicultural education comprises two sets of broad definitions: a 'conceptual' one, concerned with ways of viewing other people and the wider world, and a 'functional' one which helps us to translate the concepts into operational terms. Needless to say, the two definitions are interdependent. The value of the conceptual element is that it helps us understand the ideological bases of the different approaches that are in use, while the functional aspect is essential if the concepts are to have any real meaning at school and classroom levels. From a conceptual point of view Geneva Gay defines multicultural education as a process for:
☐ valuing individual and cultural diversity;
☐ promoting understanding of different cultural systems;
☐ developing constructive cross-cultural and inter-ethnic interaction; and
☐ achieving equality of opportunity for all children.
We can see immediately a strong overlap with the principles that we have identified already as being most central to our work. She defines the functional dimension as comprising practices and policies for:

- ☐ encouraging pupils' understanding of cultural and ethnic diversity;
- ☐ making children's home and school experiences more compatible; and
- ☐ changing the climate of the school and classroom.

Particularly important is the need to see multicultural education as consisting not only of 'content' – a body of knowledge and skills – but also of 'process' – a system for ensuring that education is delivered in a just and equitable fashion. It is as much to do with the nature of the school and classroom and the relationships within it as with the specific issues of what children are to learn.

2.   *Understanding the historical background to multicultural education and how the concept has evolved*

This involves teachers in knowing about the educational, social and political circumstances which have contributed to the development of multicultural education. Multicultural education has never been a static concept; it has evolved with changes in society and shifts of emphasis in how teachers have viewed social changes and the contribution which education can make to them. It is being suggested, then, that we should certainly be aware of different perspectives which have emerged over the years and also understand their various, often conflicting, ideological bases and the consequent variations in how teachers see the resulting classroom priorities. Numerous writers in Britain have presented their own overviews of the main strands of thought and in Chapter 1 I spent some time enlarging on Gerry Davis's ideas on the subject.[18] I would now like to draw attention to two further perspectives. Possibly the most comprehensive typology currently available to us is Alan James' *Ideologies in Multicultural Education* (see Table 2 on p. 59).[19]

A more succinct and recent view has come from Robin Richardson[20]: (see Table 3 on p. 60).

Like the James analysis this charts the evolution of thinking from the early assimilationist philosophy to the current anti-racist perspective, characterizing the policies and practices associated with each stage. It is a particularly graphic reminder for us of the polarization that has come about in recent years between the 'multiculturalists' and the 'anti-racists', a cleavage which, for reasons outlined earlier, I personally find unnecessary. However we do need to be aware of the different points of view and have the opportunity to work out our own positions. This is especially important in a primary school which is hoping to formulate a working policy for staff. In those circumstances the James and Richardson frameworks might be useful starting points for discussion.

Table 2. Ideologies in multicultural education

	Social ideology	Education ideology	Teaching methods	Curriculum content	Research preoccupations	Organization
1 Assimilation (1960s)	Absorption of minority groups into a (supposedly) homogeneous society: imperialistic paternalism	'Banking' or 'bucket-filling'	Emphasis on English as second language, 'correction' of Caribbean dialect	No modifications to traditional, ethnocentric curriculum	'Background' of immigrants, problems of cultural 'adjustment'; problems assumed to be short term	Dispersal policies, 'bussing', reception centres
2 Compensation (late 1960s)	Social democratic 'remedying' of social injustice	Compensatory	Systematic, often behaviourist, programmes for 'remediation'	Some attempts to make content 'relevant' to learner	Deficit hypothesis: minority languages and ways of life assumed to be 'disadvantages'	Remedial classes, withdrawal groups
3 Separatism (early 1970s)	Self help independent political action by minority groups: minority 'nationalism'	Knowledge as power	Pupils motivated to 'legitimate' their own identities; however, teaching mainly of the 'banking' kind	'Black studies', mother-tongue classes, etc. for minority-group pupils	Studying the structure and internal dynamics of minority groups; linguists studying language varieties, dialect	Largely 'self help' provision by the minority communities (evening and weekend classes)
4 Multicultural (mid-1970s)	Generally from the 'libertarian' left; links with other movements for 'liberating' non-standard life styles	Child centred, 'open' school	Collaborative learning, curriculum integration	Permeated by openness to all cultures; 'forms' drawn from world-wide range. Minority cultures introduced to all pupils	'Strengths' and intrinsic value of minority cultures, languages, ways of life: use of language by teachers and pupils	Responsibility on every teacher; support from resource centres, in-service courses, team teaching
5 Moral (mid-1970s)	Liberal, in its concept of a society of rational, autonomous individuals	Education as the development of rationality and moral autonomy	Open, free discussion, teacher as 'neutral chairman'; role play to foster 'empathy'	Major social issues of present day, introduced through literature, other written sources, films, pictures, etc.	Psychological and social factors causing or counteracting racism	Responsibility mainly in the 'humanities' area of the curriculum
6 Political (mid-1970s)	Socialist: racism identified as a product of class oppression	Schooling seen as 'state apparatus'; education to bring about social change	Committed teacher identifying with problems faced by (working-class, white and coloured) pupils	Emphasis on socio-political issues, but the social 'bases' of all forms of knowledge made explicit; often emphasizes local (working-class) community	Defining skills needed to fight for rights in an unjust society	Teachers and pupils involved in political organization (unions, NUSS, local community groups)

Table 3. *A map of tensions and controversies*

Assimilation	Multiculturalism	Anti-Racism
What most people still believe	*What well-meaning liberals believe*	*What genuine anti-racists believe*
Immigrants came to Britain in the 1950s and 1960s because the laws on immigration were not strict enough.	Ethnic minorities came to Britain because they had a right to and because they wanted a better life.	Black people came to Britain, as to other countries, because their labour was required by the economy.
Immigrants should integrate as quickly as possible with the British way of life.	Ethnic minorities should be able to maintain their language and cultural heritage.	Black people have to defend themselves against racist laws and practices, and to struggle for racial justice.
There is some racial prejudice in Britain, but it's only human nature, and Britain is a much more tolerant place than most other countries.	There are some misguided individuals and extremist groups in Britain, but basically our society is just and democratic, and provides equality.	Britain is a racist society and has been for several centuries. Racism is to do with power structures more than with the attitudes of individuals.
It is counter-productive to try to remove prejudice. You can't force people to like each other by bringing in laws and regulations.	Prejudice is based on ignorance and misunderstanding. It can be removed by personal contacts and the provision of information.	'Prejudice' is caused by, it is not the cause of, unjust structures and procedures. It can be removed only by dismantling these.
There should be provision of English as a second language in schools, but otherwise 'children are all children, we should treat all children exactly the same' – it is wrong to notice or emphasise cultural or racial differences.	Schools should recognise and affirm ethnic minority children's background, culture and language . . . celebrate festivals, organise international evenings, use and teach mother tongues and community languages, teach about ethnic minority history, art, music, religion, literature.	Priorities in education are for there to be more black people in positions of power and influence – as heads, senior teachers, governors, education officers, elected members; and to remove discrimination in the curriculum, classroom methods and school organisation; and to teach directly about equality and justice and against racism.

3. *Becoming familiar with the 'founders' and 'framers' of multi-cultural education*

In the same way as teachers need to be aware of the different phases in the growth of multicultural education, they should also be familiar with the individuals, organizations and publications whose work has helped extend our understanding of how education can serve cultural diversity. But first a word of caution. Primary teachers have always shown a healthy scepticism about the value of abstract academic exercises which emphasize educational theory at the expense of classroom practice. What is more, busy practitioners often do not have the time to become absorbed into the 'literature' of education. The daily needs of the classroom are usually too pressing. I am therefore very wary of making proposals which might appear to be remote from the world occupied by teachers and children. In order to clarify the situation we need to ascertain just what should be the nature of the relationship between theory and practice. Above all it should be a complementary relationship, with each working to the benefit of the other. Needless to say, this is not the traditional view, nor is it one that many teachers have. Practice is frequently seen as being in a subordinate position and having little opportunity to contribute to the development of new theoretical insights. The situation is further reinforced through an assumption that class-teachers teach whereas writers theorize, and never the twain shall meet. The relationship is therefore an uneasy one, thus, the source of many tensions. Nevertheless it is possible to make a few suggestions. First, the process of change and development in primary schools would be greatly helped if more teachers were to accept the principle of regular, informed reflection. In other words, to stand back and reflect upon the practice and policy which is so much a taken for granted part of one's professional life that it is rarely called into question. Second, teachers need to have confidence in themselves and understand that they have the capacity to think critically about educational ideas and thereby begin to develop new insights. That this can be done is evidenced by the growing number of teachers who are now becoming their own 'experts'. Writers such as John Richmond[21] have come from this self-help tradition, and so, too, have the teachers who collaborated with Clem Adelman,[22] using action research techniques to explore some of the classroom implications of racial equality. Finally, once an atmosphere of reflection and inquiry has been established teachers will be more likely to see the relevance of drawing upon writers, organizations and publications in the field[23] in order to help clarify and extend the aims and approaches which they follow.

Ethnic literacy
We make many demands of teachers and it is said that all curriculum change necessitates further demands. Responding to cultural diversity is no exception. Hardly a month goes by without the appearance of some new publication exhorting teachers to take greater account of their pupils' cultural and linguistic talents and warning of the dangers of discriminating against children through ignoring the diverse settings

in which the operate. Yet all too often overlooked is the fact that teachers may not have the knowledge and understanding necessary to honour these requests. It becomes a question of:

> . . . whether it is possible for teachers themselves, to truly respect, appreciate, and be responsive to the culturally diverse behaviours, attitudes and values of various ethnic groups if they do not understand them.[24]

'Ethnic literacy' is the term American writers often use to describe the attributes required of teachers. It can be broken down into three main aims.

1. *Understanding the way of life of different ethnic groups*
It seems fundamental that all teachers should have, as part of their essential professional knowledge, a grasp of the key features of the cultural systems of the main ethnic groups living in Britain. At a minimum level these would include awareness of languages spoken, religious beliefs, names and naming systems, dress styles and dietary habits. For teachers working in close contact with ethnic minority children a much larger data base may be needed, covering:

> . . . child-rearing practices, communication and learning styles, relational patterns, rules of etiquette and protocol, value systems, rituals, customs and traditions, family structures and relations . . .[25]

The reader will recall how attention was drawn to some of these themes as part of the earlier discussion about the manifestations of cultural diversity in the lives of individual children. At that point the focus was firmly on the children themselves, but what about the teachers who daily meet that diversity? In the main, by virtue of their upbringing in white middle class families, they are likely to have had little personal experience of living in cultural milieux where the value systems and norms of behaviour differ significantly from those of the school. It becomes all the more important, then, for teachers to be able to understand how their own taken-for-granted ground rules may be quite inapplicable to large numbers of children in their schools.

In order to illustrate this, and thereby underscore the case for teachers extending their cultural education, let us take one example. Citing research carried out in the United States by Casteñada and Ramirez, Gay discusses how children's preferred learning styles may be determined by cultural factors.[26] Most schools, she argues, operate on the principle of 'field independence' in learning, that is, they expect children to behave in an individualistic fashion and to see themselves as competitors of their peers. This is the philosophy with which most teachers have been brought up, and they often seek to perpetuate it on the 'common sense' grounds that it is what society expects: if children are not equipped with it at school, when they move into the wider world they will be seriously disadvantaged. It is also the ideology into which most white Anglo-Saxon children are inducted from their early years. Children from other cultural groups may have been socialized into a radically different set of norms. Based on 'field dependent' relationships, these will lead to the group rather than the individual being the main focus of concern with the result that such children may shy away from competitive individualism in favour of communal and group collaboration.

Whether or not these models are applicable in the British context yet remains to be fully explored, but some teachers have already reported parallel examples from their own classrooms. By way of illustration we can refer to the BBC-TV programme, 'School Report'[27] in which teachers at Birley High School, Manchester, reflect on the development of their school's multicultural education policy. At one point in the programme Loret Lee, a local Chinese community worker, talks about some of the problems which can arise for Chinese children as a result of conflicting values between home and school:

> The Chinese community, their whole livelihood and philosophy is very much based on group belonging, group consciousness and group identity. That is not to say that the society here doesn't have these sort of values, but what is less emphasised is that here, even for parliamentary democracy to work, they have to emphasise individual responsibility, individual identity and individual consciousness. Now throughout school life here you will find that there is a lot geared towards this sort of fostering and, of course, with it you have individual competitiveness as the core attitude. Chinese children are very much misunderstood at school. They may come in (to school) and say they have been helping their parents run a fish and chip shop. This would be regarded as child labour, but the Chinese community doesn't think so because this is part of them: they are contributing to a larger whole.[28]

A slight variation on the pattern is sometimes found among children of Indian origin who, though motivated by field dependency, will approach learning at school in a field independent manner. With a foot placed firmly in each camp they choose to follow the school model of individual achievement, but explain their motivation not in terms of personal gain ('it will help me find a good job') but through appeal to group loyalties ('it will please my family'). In short, cultural variables can affect children and their orientation to learning in quite divergent ways and teachers need to be informed about these in order to be able to make appropriate decisions about what to teach and how to teach it.

2. *Learning how to process information about different cultures and lifestyles*

Apart from the major problem of teachers having insufficient understanding of the cultures of different ethnic groups, problems also arise in the teachers not knowing how to process that information once acquired. There are two closely related difficulties here. The first is the ever-present danger of ethnic stereotyping: the problem of the teacher who, having acquired some rudimentary knowledge about the key cultural characteristics of a particular ethnic group, then proceeds to generalize from these into making assumptions about how all members of that group are likely to organize their lives and view the world. It is an issue which the Lifestyles project, based at the University of Nottingham, sought to address.[29] A central concern for the project team was the tendency for teachers to form judgements about other ethnic groups on the basis either of scanty information or selective interpretation of the information available. They expressed the problem in this way:

> Society is made up of a complex network of groups of which the family is, for most people, the most important. Family groups belong to wider cultural groups (religious, class, ethnic) and the attitudes and values developed within the family will be influenced by this cultural inheritance. However, human beings are active and not merely passive members of society. Consequently each family's (and each individual family member's) interpretation of the cultural inheritance will differ somewhat, so that what constitutes a family lifestyle will be in some ways similar but in other ways different to every other family. Under the pressures of everyday life and with a lack of information it is often possible to ignore these differences, and instead apply 'group' characteristics to people; however, these judgements may be naive oversimplifications or even wildly erroneous.[30]

Conversely, there is also a tendency, especially in these days of more enlightened inter-cultural attitudes, for teachers to dismiss as stereotyping any attempts to specify the cultural traits of particular ethnic groups, or simply to refuse to accept the validity of any group cultural profile. Geneva Gay illustrates the point thus:

> . . . in the process of examining Mexican American learning styles if the observation is made that members of this group tend to prefer co-operative, group-based learning modes to competitive individualistic ones, the inclination is for some teachers to respond thus:

> 'But not all Mexican Americans are like that'. Or, 'You're stereotyping Mexican American students'. Or, 'I know some Anglos, Blacks, Slavs and Native Americans who behave the same way.'[31]

Observations of this nature, albeit with different ethnic examples, are becoming increasingly common among teachers in Britain and I have to say that I find it quite refreshing. It is encouraging that teachers are now more cautious when it comes to condensing the complex identities of ethnic minority groups into a collection of anodyne statements to fit the cultural dictionary. Yet, at the same time, many ethnic groups do have their own cultural distinctiveness which often gives rise to identifiable patterns of behaviour, sets of beliefs and values. An essential skill for the teacher lies in being able to combine an awareness of these characteristic features with a sensitive knowledge of individual children and their families, in such a way as to avoid bland sweeping generalizations.

3. *Understanding the presence and influence of ethnic minority groups in the shaping of British history, life and culture*
At one level this is a priority within the informational resources which teachers have available to inform their work in the classroom. It encompasses several needs:
   □ to understand the reasons for immigration to Britain;
   □ to know about the history of people from black and other minorities in Britain;
   □ to see Britain not as a recently multiculturalized society but as having a long tradition of diversity;
   □ to recognize the contribution to science, medicine, politics and other fields of human endeavour made by men and women from non-European backgrounds;
   □ to be aware of how ordinary men and women from ethnic minority groups have contributed to life in Britain.
At another level it means that we all have to become aware of the subtle yet pervasive ways in which our own educational background and social upbringing have led us to a mono-cultural outlook on the world and an inclination to devalue the shaping influence which people from other ethnic groups have had on it. The legacy of Empire Day celebrations in the school playground, atlases dominated by expanses of pink and stories of great white explorers and discoverers is difficult to shake off. So it is hardly surprising that we still have a tendency to view and explain race-related events from a white standpoint. We are inclined to think of the achievements of human kind as being the exclusive claim of Europeans – and male Europeans at that. Consequently, when confronted with a black interpretation of events, our reaction is likely to be one of indignation and resistance. What is called for, then, is something more than a broadening of the data base from which we operate, important though that is: we need to develop a sharper awareness of how our assumptions and beliefs are

products of the backgrounds we have known, and, in addition, an ability to evaluate ourselves and become more conscious of how we are thinking and behaving.

Professional applications

Thus far the discussion has been confined to identifying the principles, skills and body of knowledge which are prerequisites for teaching in a culturally diverse society. We now turn to the professional applications.

1. *Translating knowledge about multicultural education and cultural diversity into classroom practice*

There is a tendency for us to assume that, once the content of teaching has been agreed, the process of putting it into practice will take care of itself. I am suggesting something different, since my own experience is that teachers require and appreciate as much support at the application stage as at the earlier one where the concept and components of multicultural education are being introduced. A strategy which is in quite widespread use nowadays, as part of school-based professional development programmes, is for teachers to be encouraged to devise and try out with children a small curriculum unit based on the insights they have gained. In the primary school this unit could take one of several forms. One might be a theme focused on some aspect of cultural, ethnic or linguistic diversity and designed to permeate several curriculum areas. Alternatively it might be based not so much on curriculum content, but more on the process of learning. An example here would include trying out different techniques for handling classroom discussion,[32] possibly concerning some current race-related event, a topical issue in the local community, or an incident of racist behaviour in which children have been involved. Having put their ideas into practice teachers then often find it valuable to discuss with other colleagues what they actually did, where they see it developing, and how the children responded.

A further way of helping teachers to reflect on their practice is through making videotape recordings of them at work and using these as a basis for discussion afterwards. But there is a problem here, since teachers are inclined to see the act of teaching as an essentially private affair between themselves and their pupils. They might be willing to discuss their initiatives with colleagues but the idea of going on public view is still, for many, an intimidating prospect. Whilst such sensitivities should be respected, we need to understand that putting multicultural ideals into practice does not simply involve changing curriculum content, important though that is. Rather, the process by which the curriculum is mediated to children is equally important. A topic badly taught remains a badly taught topic, irrespective of how rich it might be in cultural diversity. Of course, many would argue, myself included, that cultural diversity can be a powerful motivator for children, and can engage their interest in a way that other curriculum *foci* often may not. But this in itself will not cancel out the effect of poor teaching. What is more, if a diversity-related topic were to fail in the classroom through inappropriate teaching styles it might blight further multicultural initiatives. In other words, then, when translating knowledge about multicultural education and cultural diversity into actuality, teachers should not suspend their normal professional judgement about what constitutes good educational practice.

2. *Acquiring the ability to analyse and clarify one's own values, attitudes, expectations and behaviour towards ethnically different groups and individuals*

It comes as something of a shock to teachers to be told that, as a consequence of growing up in a society which has inherent inequalities and racist characteristics, they – and indeed all of us from the white majority – are likely to harbour attitudes and ways of behaving which are prejudicial towards people from minority groups. But what can teachers do about this? How can teachers learn to 'become observant, analytical interpreters of their own racial, ethnic and social attitudes and behaviour, understanding how and when these are liable to surface in the classroom, and developing techniques for controlling and/or changing them'?[33] This is not the point at which to enter into a lengthy discourse on the strategies for attitudinal and behavioural change that abound at the present time, except to say that, like the broader debate on multicultural education, these fall into two seemingly irreconcilable camps. The first, based on social psychological research about attitude change, involves, in the words of Ken Thomas, one of the authors of the 'Lifestyles' materials[34] which probably best typify the approach: 'the creation of an atmosphere in which teachers can openly and honestly discuss their feelings and beliefs with the risks of confrontation minimized'.[35] Brief reference was made earlier to the 'Lifestyles' pack but the following extract from the users' guide provides a clearer picture of what is entailed:

The Workshop Activity
(a) *Preparation*
At the beginning of the activity participants are provided with some basic information about a particular family, and are invited to make intelligent

guesses about the opinions that members of the family might hold with regard to a number of aspects of family life (for example, their attitudes to marriage).

These 32 topics are displayed on eight layout strips as a basis for this guesswork, and an 'opinion bank' is provided.

The opinions bank contains sets of cards, each set corresponding to the various *topics*; and each set of cards indicates a range of possible *opinions* with regard to each particular topic.

In addition, a blank card is included in each set, in order that participants can indicate a fresh opinion if they do not think that the rest of the opinions in the set are adequate.

(b) *How the activity starts*

Participants work in small sub-groups or syndicates. They select from each set which they believe would represent the opinions of the family, and place them on the layout strip.

The whole group is then invited to peruse all the opinion cards on the strips and to indicate any disagreement by turning a card face down. Preliminary discussion of any areas of disagreement can then begin either in sub-groups or within the group as a whole.

(c) *How the activity continues*

Up till now, participants have been exchanging personal opinions. At an appropriate point, however, additional information is provided in the form of an envelope which contains a selection of materials provided by an actual family: snapshots of them at home, at work, at leisure, a shopping list; a week's menus; a page from a diary or a letter to a friend; comments on past, present or possible future issues of concern to the family; statements of belief; and so on.

The members of the workshop group pass these materials amongst themselves, and in the light of this new information, they discuss changes they would like to make in the opinions they have placed on the layout strips, or areas of disagreement they would now like to indicate. Further discussion on the areas of disagreement can then also take place.

Whereas previously the group had been speculating on the opinions of the family in the light of their existing knowledge of that particular 'type' of family, they are now led to compare notes about this real family. There might well be disagreement about the extent to which individual items contained in the envelope of additional information indicate the family's opinions in a number of areas. But in the course of discussing these areas of disagreement, differing interpretations of the significance of these items are likely to emerge which may lead participants to modify earlier assumptions.

(d) *The final stages*

Once the group has completed this reassessment a sealed envelope, which contains the family's *own* opinions with regard to the various topics, is opened. In the light of this third input of information the participants may well have to reconsider their views yet again. In so doing they may well come to see the family not as a stereotype but as one pursuing its own

individual lifestyle, in some ways similar to and in other ways different
from all other families in contemporary Britain.

The second approach is usually known as 'Race Awareness Training'.
Closely influenced by the work of the American writer, Judy Katz,[36]
this is more explicit in its intentions. It is described by John Twitchin,
producer of the BBC-TV series 'Case Studies in Multicultural
Education'[37] and himself a prominent figure in the field, as having
three aims:

> To offer an opportunity to explore our own feelings and attitudes with
> regard to racism;
> To gain an understanding of the nature and effects of institutional racism;
> To measure how we check institutional racism in ourselves, in our work.[38]

We see these ideas at work in 'Teacher, Examine Thyself!', programme 6 of the BBC series. Here, a group of Bradford teachers 'who
are already sensitized to multicultural approaches'[39] are seen taking
part, over a two-day period, in a number of activities intended to help
them 'discover . . . how much school practice is at best unwittingly
patronizing or tokenist, or at worst, unintentionally racist . . .'.[40] At
the core of the exercise is an activity that involves the teachers
inventing 'a school system deliberately designed to be subtly racist:
defined in the sense of preserving in practice a white majority's
advantages over a black minority in a society which in theory
outlawed discrimination and held publicly to principles of equal
opportunity for all'.[41] Not surprisingly, the teachers soon realize that
the school system they know, including as it does initiatives in
multicultural education, is strikingly similar to the one they have
invented. Since the BBC series, training courses of this sort have
become far more widespread, with several LEAs incorporating them
into their own in-service programmes. Nevertheless the approach
remains contentious, on account of its emphasis on uncovering the
racism inherent in the beliefs and assumptions on which we base our
views of the world in an emotionally challenging fashion.

When deciding which approach to take we find ourselves in a
polarized, forced-choice situation, very similar to that which
emerged in our earlier discussion of the multicultural and anti-racist
perspectives on the curriculum. At that time I took the view that the
two outlooks are not mutually exclusive. Let us recall the argument.
The celebration of diversity, I maintained, will in itself offer little to
children's life chances unless accompanied by an anti-racist commitment to equality of opportunity. Similarly I argued that the anti-
racist focus on challenging the inequity of the education system will
have only limited impact unless the curriculum reflects the diversity of

experience which goes to make up our multicultural society. The same argument should apply here, too. Teachers need to be sensitized to variations within and between cultures, but they need also to be aware of how their own beliefs and expectations, mirroring those of the wider society, can result in ways of behaving which are prejudicial to children from ethnic minority groups. Perhaps the modus operandi should be that in the early stages, when teachers are beginning to think about cultural diversity and its implications for education, a subtle awareness-raising strategy, like 'Lifestyles', may be most appropriate. But as teachers' experience grows, so too does their readiness to evaluate their practice critically and look closely into their own attitudes. It is at this level that the race awareness programmes may have most to offer.

3. *Developing appropriate teaching styles and professional methods of working*

To talk about adopting 'appropriate' styles of working in schools may appear presumptuous, since it presupposes not only that some styles are 'less appropriate' and others 'more appropriate' but also that it is right to intrude on teachers' traditional autonomy in deciding their own preferred methods of operating. Over recent years there has been a strong trend among LEAs toward laying down precise guidelines on the content of children's learning in respect of cultural diversity. Similarly with national projects; witness, for instance, the Schools Council's *Education for A Multiracial Society: Curriculum and Context 5–13*,[42] which formulated concrete proposals about the ideas and knowledge which schools should aim to transmit to children. By comparison, as pointed out earlier, the 'process' aspect of learning, notably the teaching methods used, has received scant attention. Indeed the Schools Council project seemed consciously to eschew any involvement with the process dimension:

> The aspect of the formal curriculum that receives most attention (in the report) is its content – the facts, ideas and themes that make it up and the materials servicing them. In striking this emphasis, the project finds itself slightly at odds with child-centred educational theory, and with other recent curriculum projects for the same age range which stress process rather than content.[43]

The assumption seems to be that once the content has been adjusted, the process of putting it into effect will take care of itself. I suggest this is a mistaken assumption, for if the teaching and learning processes are ignored, teachers may tend to rely on the methods with which they feel most secure, and the evidence of recent years seems to suggest that these are more akin to the didactic transmission-oriented styles of their own schooling than the child-centred approaches popularly associated with primary schools.[44] Here it might be helpful to note the characteristics of the didactic model and, thereby, highlight its limitations for teaching about cultural diversity. To do this we can turn to Stephen Rowland. He says this about didactic teaching:

> The aim is to instil certain pre-specified skills or knowledge in the student. The teacher imparts instruction (either directly or through programmed learning packages), the student responds; the teacher marks, and further instructions follow.[45]

For him, this traditional style has many limitations but by far the most significant of these, and one that is of relevance to us in our present discussion, is that:

> Such a basis for educating the young may be suitable as a means for conditioning the next generation to the needs of society as perceived by the teacher. But can it educate them for a future society in which they will play a critical, responsible and self-determining role?[46]

So, Stephen Rowland would argue that didactic teaching restricts children's capacity for thinking critically about ideas and events that they encounter. To this we could add that it does little to create the ethos of hospitality in the classroom which is essential if children are to be able to demonstrate their own cultural and linguistic resources and to share in the resources of others.

Alternative, and I would suggest, more appropriate methods of working have been coming to the fore over a number of years. Stephen Rowland himself has much to say about these and we shall return to his work again in some detail in Chapter 5, when attention is turned more closely to the classroom. We can also learn a great deal from the pioneering work of Douglas Barnes[47] which pointed to the potential of group learning techniques as means of enabling children's undeclared talents and skills to come to the surface in the classroom. Teachers working with him found that pupils' group discussions 'displayed a quality that far exceeded the calibre of their contributions in class', that in groups children 'manifested unexpected skills and competences'.[48] The findings came as a surprise to many teachers, which fact in itself must be linked to teachers' assumptions and expectations about what children are capable of doing. For, as Barnes argues, traditionally schooling has presented pupils as the passive receivers of learning: 'Teachers know, but pupils do not – if they do, they know imperfectly'.[49] He goes on to point out that we have assumed that if children are to achieve a deeper knowledge and understanding it will only be possible under the teacher's direct guidance and control. In saying this he has no wish to deny the importance and necessity of the teacher, nor to suggest that small groups in themselves offer the panacea, but it is very clear that children's skills and competences are often underestimated and rarely called upon in the conventional classroom. We know from studies of classroom interaction[50] that it is usually teachers who manage and control the discourse. Not only do they do most of the talking but they also assume responsibility for the content, pacing and style of pupils' contributions. They decide on the topic to be discussed; they ask questions to which they already know the answers; they nominate who is to speak; and so on. When the relationship is reversed, however, responsibility devolves on to the children. They have to negotiate who contributes, when and how. They have to assume the overall monitoring role. Not surprisingly, the quality of the discourse can change dramatically and, equally signific-ant for our present discussion, so too can the subject matter.

It is my contention that the interactive-collaborative approach is most compatible with the idea of children learning about cultural variety. I say this for three reasons. First, in the multicultural school this approach is the only productive arrangement whereby children of ethnically and linguistically varied backgrounds are able to discuss their diverse experiences and learn from each other. Second, it is potentially the most supportive arrangement for children to explore their feelings on questions of race, culture and language. Finally, in reversing the traditional teacher-pupil relationship, it enables the teacher to take on a learning role vis-à-vis his or her pupils without feeling threatened or undermined.

It would be blinkered to assume that an interactive-collaborative policy should be confined to the teacher-pupil relationship. Rather, its implications should extend to the school as a whole, including the professional relationships between teachers themselves. We all have much to learn from each other, and if the school is to develop a coherent response to the multicultural society professional collabor-ation is not just desirable but absolutely essential. This collaboration should certainly entail closer co-operation between class teacher colleagues, through a regular pooling of ideas and insights and a collective approach to common problems. And, just as important, it should envisage a more prominent and active classroom-based role for support teachers, whether specialists in ESL teaching or bi-lingualism.

A further dimension to the approach involves teachers moving beyond the school to link up with the resources embodied in their pupils' families and communities. I would hesitate to suggest that teachers seek to 'use' the expertise of their local communities, as the connotations of 'using' people are quite unsavoury. In one sense it is simply a question of finding ways of enlisting community support. But if the notion of partnership, which the collaborative philosophy implies, is to be adhered to the relationship should entail more than parents giving of themselves. They should be able to expect that their giving of support to the school will be reciprocated by an invitation to discuss with the teachers the education which their children are receiving.

4. *Knowing how to evaluate the school climate, curriculum and resources*

Geneva Gay contends that, in the final analysis, the effectiveness of any commitment to multicultural education will reflect the degree to which it permeates all aspects of the school: interpersonal relations, organization, decision making, policy objectives, resources and programmes of work. To make assessments of any of these obviously calls for some system of evaluation. We might argue, therefore, that one of the priorities for the teacher is to acquire the skills necessary to be able to participate in this evaluation. In many primary schools self-evaluation is gradually being accepted as an integral part of each teacher's professional responsibilites. As a result, many schools have now devised their own checklists to be used by individual teachers to monitor their classroom work. Similarly, at the whole-school level, it is not unusual nowadays for a primary school to have a procedure whereby each member of staff, possibly once or twice a year, produces his or her own appraisal of the school, highlighting areas of need in terms of policy, resources, organization and classroom practice, and for these individual evaluations to be followed up with whole staff discussions where future priorities are identified and strategies of working agreed. Such an approach serves the twin purpose of helping to equip class teachers with the skills necessary for reviewing their own practice whilst involving the staff as a whole in collective reflection on the school.

As a next step we now need to extend these procedures and the checklists used so as to incorporate more precise guidelines on how the school might educate its pupils for cultural diversity. Probably one of the more searching and comprehensive checklists available for school use is that produced by the Berkshire LEA.[51] It consists of a series of questions designed to help teachers to see the links between their day-to-day practice and the authority's policy on Education for Racial Equality. The policy itself is based on six general principles, that is:

Berkshire County Council requires and supports all its educational institutions and services to create, maintain and promote racial equality and justice.

The Council is opposed to racism in all its forms. It wishes therefore:

1. To promote understanding of the principles and practices of racial equality and justice, and commitment to them.
2. To identify and remove all practices, procedures and customs which discriminate against ethnic minority people and to replace them with procedures which are fair to all.
3. To encourage ethnic minority parents and communities to be fully involved in the decision-making processes which affect the education of their children.
4. To increase the influence of ethnic minority parents, organisations and communities by supporting educational and cultural projects which they themselves initiate.
5. To encourage the recruitment of ethnic minority teachers, administrators and other staff at all levels, and the appointment of ethnic minority governors.
6. To monitor and evaluate the implementation of County Council policies, and to make changes and corrections as appropriate.

Within the document each of these principles is taken as a discussion theme and broken down into a checklist of questions. Space does not allow the whole document to be reproduced,[52] but to illustrate how a theme is presented in a form which can be readily interpreted at school level let us consider principle number 1:

1.1   Concepts and themes

Which topics in primary schools, and which subjects and syllabuses in secondary schools, are most relevant for developing understanding of racial equality and justice? For example, when and where at our school are pupils likely to be learning, directly or indirectly, about concepts or themes such as the following:

(i) Diversity: both in Britain and in world society there is a variety of cultures, beliefs, customs, systems, priorities.

(ii) Similarity: human beings have basic physical needs in common, for example nutrition, shelter and health, and all pursue values such as security, dignity and self-respect.

(iii) Justice: relationships and procedures should be fair as distinct from discriminatory, and disputes and conflicts should be resolved on moral and legal principles, not through power alone.

(iv) Civilisation: great achievements in law, politics, science, technology, the arts, have been made through history in many different countries and cultures, not in Europe alone.

(v) Migration: throughout history human beings have migrated from one country to another, though for different reasons at different times; in the 1950s and 1960s migration to Western Europe was required in particular for economic reasons.

(vi) Racism: discriminatory systems and practices, and the prejudices which they both reflect and strengthen, need to be identified and understood, and should be opposed both for moral reasons and self-interest reasons.

(vii) Colonialism: relationships and beliefs in the contemporary world are of course influenced by the past; it is particularly important in this regard to understand European exploration and expansion from the sixteenth century onwards, and to see these from Third World viewpoints as well as from European ones.

(viii) Resistance: struggles and campaigns against injustice take various forms, with regard for example to styles of leadership, the use of existing laws, the use of force, the pace of change, the degree of eventual success.

(ix) Interdependence: each neighbourhood and town in modern Britain, as also modern Britain as a whole, is part of 'one world' – a single world society and economy, whose various parts continually influence each other.

1.2 Textbooks
To what extent do our textbooks and other learning materials reflect the concepts and themes mentioned above? Have we systematically reviewed the textbooks and other materials in our classrooms, stores, resource collections and library, in order to remove those which are an actual hindrance to the teaching of these concepts?

1.3 Displays
Do displays of pupils' work in classrooms, corridors and the school foyer reflect recurring attention to these concepts and themes? Do posters and wall-charts in these places similarly reflect these concepts and themes?

1.4 General ethos
In what ways, and to what extents, do learning and teaching methods in classrooms promote and require active cooperation and collaboration amongst pupils as equals? In what ways do pastoral arrangements and general school organisation promote understanding of fairness and equality?

1.5 Combating racialism
Do all staff both teaching and non-teaching, have an explicit and consistent policy against racialist insults, remarks and assaults by pupils; condemning and removing racialist grafitti and propaganda; and condemning and counteracting the activities of racialist organisations in the school neighbourhood?

1.6 Responsibility
Is there a member of staff, or a staff working party, responsible for ensuring that the curriculum for all pupils includes attention to concepts relating to racial equality and justice?

Often one finds that statements of policy remain at such a level of generality that teachers simply do not understand what they are supposed to do about them. It is almost assumed that the mere exhortation to implement ideals of racial equality will result in teachers conceptualizing the classroom implications. The Berkshire document is exceptional. Notice how it speaks directly to the practitioner through a series of key questions, each of which touches in very tangible terms on some aspect of school life. Notice also how the document does not differentiate between themes which are mainly the concern of the teacher and those which are at the level of school policy-making. Rather, it prefers to work from an assumption that the two strands are interdependent: what happens in the classroom is influenced, if not determined, by policy decisions about staffing, resources and organization; equally, teachers will only be confident about policy decisions if they are seen to connect with classroom experience and to reflect the corporate viewpoint of staff.

These are questions which we shall be pursuing in more detail later; at this stage we should summarize the present chapter's main concerns before moving on in Chapter 4 to community-related themes.

Summary
In this chapter we have:
1. reviewed some of the evidence which shows that teachers are inclined to form expectations of children on the basis of ethnic and social stereotypes;
2. summarized some of the findings which show how these expectations are likely to influence teachers' classroom behaviour towards children and, in turn, affect children's performance in school;
3. referred to investigations of the past ten years which suggest that, in multicultural schools, despite a growing awareness of the need for a diversity-based approach to learning, assimilationist beliefs continue to exist among teachers;
4. argued, again from research studies, that the prevailing atmosphere in all-white schools is one of indifference, even hostility, towards the idea of a multicultural curriculum for their pupils;
5. offered a framework for the main areas of knowledge and interpersonal and professional skills which teachers need to be developing.

Further reading
It is important to be aware of the critiques of the teacher-expectations thesis, and a sound review of these is contained in Nash, R. (1976) *Teacher Expectations and Pupil Learning*, Routledge and Kegan

Paul. Words of caution are also voiced in the Swann Report, Chapter 3, 'Achievement and Underachievement'. The different ideological perspectives on multicultural education are given a balanced and thorough treatment in the Open University Course E354, Block 4. The idea of teachers becoming more critically aware of what is taking place in their own classrooms is covered by several writers, but a multicultural perspective on this is given by Adelman, C. et al (1983) *A Fair Hearing For All*, Bulmershe College, and Nixon, J. (1985) *A Teacher's Guide to Multicultural Education*, Basil Blackwell. Valuable training aids for reviewing attitudes and assumptions are Schools Council (1983) *Nottingham University Lifestyles Pack*, Nottingham University School of Education, and 'Teacher Examine Thyself', a programme in the BBC-TV series, *Case Studies in Multicultural Education.*

4 Community perspectives

It is common nowadays to talk of the child's educational development as involving a three-way triangular relationship between child, teacher and parent. So far, we have examined our diversity theme from the points of view of the first two partners in this relationship. It remains to complete the triangle by focusing on the parent or, perhaps more appropriately, on the community of which the parent is a part.

Already a number of themes have emerged which need to be examined further. The reader will recall how in Chapter 2 attention was drawn to the expectations of ethnic minority parents for their children's development as reflected in their communities' efforts to provide for children's learning. At that point, our interest was in the contribution of community, or supplementary schools in maintaining a sense of cultural and linguistic cohesion among children. These schools, however, have another role: of providing a supplementary educational service – and this stems directly from a loss of confidence in some aspects of the mainstream sector. There are other issues, too. Much has been said in recent years about the need for dialogue between school and home. Yet beyond the level of exhortation there is little evidence of how educators in a multi-ethnic setting have sought to unravel the complexities of this. Allied with the need for dialogue is the current debate about the school's accountability to its local community, with all the tensions that such an issue highlights. And, of course, at the primary phase especially, there is the continuing discussion, with its origins in the Plowden Report, about the contribution which parents can make to children's learning, which has drawn renewed vigour from recent trends towards involving parents in children's reading development. These issues will be the main *foci* for this chapter.

Parents and their children's education
In primary schools, so much of what we now take for granted as representing good practice in terms of forging closer links between home and school can be traced back to the Plowden Report[1] of 1967.

Home visiting, Open Days, Information Booklets, community use of school facilities, all these were among the recommendations which the report made and to which many schools responded imaginatively and enthusiastically.[2] The report's underlying thinking, however, was firmly within what subsequently became known as the 'deficit model', a tradition which, among other things, promoted an image of working class parents as lacking the skills and knowledge necessary to provide a home environment supportive towards educational achievement. Put crudely, it was thought that working class children were failing at school because of the impoverished nature of their cultural backgrounds. By contrast, middle class homes were thought to operate on a value system akin to that of the school: similar modes of language were used, books and educational materials were available in plentiful supply, and education itself was highly prized.

In the ensuing years, however, a number of writers were critical of the Plowden view,[3] and before long evidence began to emerge showing that working class parents, far from being apathetic about their children's development, were often taking their own steps to give support and encouragement in the home. John and Elizabeth Newson, for instance, in a study of working class parents in Nottingham[4], showed that over 80 per cent of those interviewed were actively helping their children with reading. More recently the work of Barbara Tizard[5] and Gordon Wells[6] has offered up strong evidence to show that working class homes are not the linguistically impoverished environments of the deficit tradition and in fact offer children numerous opportunities for stimulation and interaction.

Since Plowden, by far the largest investigation into the involvement of parents in primary schools was undertaken by the National Foundation for Educational Research in the late 1970s.[7] Over 1,600 schools throughout England and Wales were involved and between them they reported a wide range of parental involvement activities (see Table 4 overleaf), which led the researchers concerned to conclude that schools were progressing, albeit cautiously, towards the Plowden Committee's recommendations.[8]

In terms of our present discussion, however, another aspect of the survey's findings may be equally important: many teachers perceived parents' involvement in education as a threat to their professional status. The fear seemed to be that parents, who were essentially amateurs in the educational business, were becoming increasingly involved with the education of children and in so doing were causing the skills which teachers themselves had developed through professional training and experience to become devalued. This particular dimension of the discussion will assume greater importance as the

Table 4. *Parental involvement activities*

Type of Involvement	Percentage of Primary Schools
Parents help on school visits and outings.	78
Parents do sewing (e.g., costumes for Christmas play) and minor repairs to school equipment.	65
Parents provide transport for football, etc., matches at other schools.	54
Parents with specialist knowledge (e.g., local policeman, fireman, etc.) give talks to children.	45
Parents help with craft work, cooking, music, etc., under supervision of teacher.	36
Parents help in school library, covering books, etc.	29
Parents hear children read under supervision of teacher.	26
Parents help with football, after-school clubs, etc.	22
Parents help dress children after P.E. or swimming.	20
Parents help generally in classroom, putting out materials, cleaning up at end of day, etc.	19
Parents do major repairs and/or alterations to school buildings (e.g., turn cloakrooms into classrooms).	10
Parents run or help with holiday play scheme.	7
Parents run a library scheme for the school	4

focus is now narrowed from consideration of parents generally to ethnic minority parents in particular.

Ethnic minority parents
As with working class parents, there has been a widespread assumption that ethnic minority families are indifferent towards their children's education. Yet there is little shortage of evidence to the contrary. The main study from which to draw is that of Rex and Tomlinson[9] conducted in 1976 among 700 ethnic minority and 400 white 'British' parents in the Handsworth area of Birmingham. On the specific point of parental interest in education the writers concluded that:

> . . . contrary to widespread beliefs that some minority group parents do not take much interest in their children's education, our study indicated that not only do they take great interest, but both West Indian and Asian parents have made particular efforts to understand a complex and unfamiliar system, and they have high expectations of school.[10]

Among Asian and West Indian parents little evidence was found of parental apathy, indeed a majority of those questioned had visited their child's school at some time during the preceding six months, often making a special visit outside the normal Open Day and Parents' Evening opportunities. Similar findings emerged from a study by Ghuman[11] of Sikh parents; and in a recent study by Tomlinson[12] ethnic minority parents are shown to have a strong commitment towards supporting their children's education both as something which is intrinsically worthwhile and a key to success in the wider society.

This is not the complete story. Each of the studies I have mentioned also uncovered among parents grave dissatisfaction with the education being offered to their children. For Afro-Caribbean parents this dissatisfaction had its roots in schools failing to provide the 'equality of opportunity' which they had long expected. In short, black children were underachieving and the schools were responsible. Among Asian parents frustration was just as strong, only in their case it arose from the schools' failure to provide adequately for their cultures, languages and religious practices. Thus John Rex,[13] in evidence to the Swann Committee, was able to summarize the main concerns of Asian parents as including provision for 'mother tongue classes' and 'specific issues relating to school assemblies, food, dress and sex segregation'. It is against this background of belief in the value of education but loss of confidence in the mainstream system's ability to deliver equal and appropriate educational opportunities to their children, that we should view the moves by black and Asian communities towards establishing their own supplementary schooling.

Supplementary schooling
In Chapter 2 attention was drawn to the work of community-run schools which had been born out of a desire by ethnic minority parents to maintain cultural, religious and linguistic attributes for their children. Other supplementary schools, especially those run by Afro-Caribbean communities, are more directly critical of the mainstream system and exist not just to provide cultural input but to equip children with skills and abilities which, they feel, are otherwise denied them. The most penetrating discussion of this aspect of community education has come from Maureen Stone[14] to whom brief reference was made in Chapter 3. Now is the time to expand on her arguments, for they go to the heart of the issue of the relations between schools and ethnic minority communities. Widespread within the West Indian community, she maintains, is 'real bitterness' that weekday schools are 'short-changing the kids', that black children are 'illiterate and innumerate' because they are not being given the intensive attention they need. In short:

. . . the West Indian community generally regards the school system as

reinforcing and sanctioning the racist views which exist in society at large
and which regard people of African descent as basically inferior to people
of European descent.[15]

Supplementary or Saturday schools, she argues, are a product of this
bitterness and demonstrate the community's belief in its own capacity
to bring about improvement. Their approach is based on a commitment to values of 'hard work, high aspirations and willingness to
sacrifice', and thus, Stone continues, they represent a distinct break
with the 'vague affective-type goals' of the mainstream system which
emphasize 'self-concept, self-esteem and enjoyment . . . at the
expense of more concrete objectives'.

While not dismissing the importance of children enjoying school
and having a positive view of themselves, Stone maintains that these
ideals should not be promoted at the expense of the 'mastery of skills
and knowledge and the development of abilities'. Moreover her own
research leads her to conclude that children attending Saturday
schools, where such traditional values are emphasized, are more likely
than others to display a positive self-image and commitment to the
very notion of education. Thus she moves to her central recommendation, that West Indian children should be taught by the formal
methods of the supplementary sector. For it is only these methods that
can lead to an improvement in attainment whilst carrying the
confidence of black parents.

Emerging issues

To the primary teacher who is committed to the principle of a child-
centred, broadly-based curriculum, Maureen Stone's view of learning
will appear narrow and instrumental. Similarly disturbing will be the
demands from some sections of the Muslim community for segregation of boys and girls. Both will be seen to be akin to a tradition from
which primary schools have sought to distance themselves over the
past 20 years, and it is feared that if they were to be adopted they
would have the effect of stifling the creativity and innovatory
techniques which underpin so much of primary practice.

Presented in such stark terms there is no doubt that Stone's
propositions would run counter to much of what primary education
stands for. But set in the wider context of many ethnic minority
parents' clear dissatisfaction with the curriculum of their children's
schools they can be seen as posing questions which teachers must at
some time address. In short, they relate to some fundamental issues:
What opportunity do parents have to find out about the work of the
school? Does the ethos of the school encourage parents to become
involved with their children's learning? What consultation has taken

place with parents about the curriculum and practice of the school? Are parents able to express their views about aspects of the school's work? Are their views taken into account when decisions are being made? It is these issues which we need to consider in more detail as we move on to examine some of the practical strategies that teachers might employ when seeking to develop a coherent programme for fostering closer relations between school and community.

Stages in developing school/community relations
Cherry Fulloway, a Leicestershire Primary Head with strong experience of working in multicultural schools, describes ten stages which her present school passed through in developing its community orientation.[16] These are set out in Figure 2 overleaf. It is rare for practitioners to be able to examine their own practices and experiences in such a systematic and dispassionate manner. I therefore intend to make use of her statement as a basis for furthering the discussion. Before doing so, however, a number of points need to be made. First, although Fulloway talks about stages of development she would stress that these stages are at no time discrete. Equally, she would stress that development in her school did not take place in an unhindered linear fashion. Rather, the process, as with most educational change, was more of a spiral, with no shortage of setbacks and with much time being spent in reflection and consolidation. Finally, it is not suggested that the experience she describes should be seen as a blueprint to which other teachers should slavishly adhere. Quite the contrary. Each school will evolve its own route and stages as a result of the circumstances in which it finds itself. But it is hoped that the experience of other teachers will be of help in planning lines of development and assessing progress. With these caveats, I offer the ten-point framework (Figure 2) as a basis for constructing the type of checklist for self-appraisal and action which was set out in Chapter 2 when considering teachers' professional development.

Written communication of information
Primary schools have long relied on the printed word as a principal means of communication with parents and in recent years the volume of paper being sent from school to home has increased considerably. A major reason for this has been the 1980 Education Act[17] with its legal requirement that all schools produce a written document setting out details of admission arrangements, curriculum policies, organizational procedures, governors and teaching staff. Given this plethora of printed matter it is vital that schools become more conscious of the nature and effectiveness of the communication that is taking place.

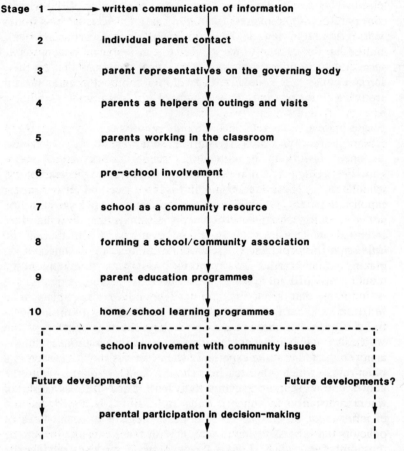

Figure 2
STAGES IN DEVELOPING SCHOOL/COMMUNITY RELATIONS

Questions need to be asked about the style of written documents: Is the text clear? Can it be misunderstood? Is it tactful? Is it too complex and detailed? Does it rely on jargon? Equally important, schools need to become more aware of the 'hidden curriculum' of their written communication, the covert messages which are being transmitted to readers. John Bastiani makes a salutary point:

> Throughout the range of written forms of contact, schools reveal a great deal of themselves, often more than they realise, and sometimes more than they mean to.[18]

So, even when a school may publicly declare its commitment to closer liaison with its community the form and style of its circulars may convey a very different message, and there is little doubt that parents will register this and draw their own conclusions. In schools serving multi-ethnic neighbourhoods the issue becomes yet more complex, since here, to be effective, written communications should take account of the bilingualism of many of their intended readers. There are two points to be made. The first is a purely practical one. Some parents, though sufficiently proficient in English for everyday purposes, might have difficulty coping with the written form of communication and will therefore feel more comfortable if the documents they receive have been translated into the language they know best. The second is more ideological and goes to the heart of the school's policy towards its community. If we insist on all communication with parents taking place through the medium of English we are not just placing some families at a disadvantage, but are also effectively declaring that we hold the community's linguistic skills in little regard. By contrast, the school that communicates bilingually is making a clear statement of support for diversity and is laying a sound foundation for future relationships.[19]

Communication, however, is not solely dependent on the written word. Indeed there seems to be something peculiarly Western about the preoccupation with print. Other cultures place much greater emphasis on oral communication and it is this tradition that binds many ethnic minority communities together in Britain. Yet schools so often remain unaware of its significance. They know little about the network systems at work within their local communities, the places where informal contact occurs and the individuals who are the sources of information to whom others turn. If a school's communication policy is to be fully effective, then, less conventional channels than those hitherto used also need to be explored. Home visits will take on greater importance as will other informal opportunities for contact. Above all, the key ingredient is the school's willingness to step beyond its own walls and meet members of its community on their own territory and on their terms.

Individual parent contact
For parents of primary age children there are probably three types of situation where contact takes place between them and their children's teachers. The first comes with the child's admission to school. Then, at carefully spaced intervals in the child's school career, there are likely to be opportunities to attend Open Days or Parents' Evenings in order to see the child's work and discuss his or her progress with the class teacher. Other occasions are often problem-centred, involving parent

and teacher meeting together to consider some difficulty that has arisen.

Admission arrangements vary greatly, but they are often very effective channels for conveying impressions of the school and its teachers to parents. If these impressions are to be positive and lay the ground for a continuing relationship the school needs to be critically aware of its policy. The following questions touch upon some of the key issues:

☐ Who does the school admissions? Is there someone who can act as interpreter?
☐ What information is gathered?
☐ Does it include details of the language(s) spoken by the child, parents and siblings?
☐ Are admission forms multilingual? Are they sent out or given to parents in advance?
☐ What is the school policy on names?
☐ How are they pronounced and written?
☐ Does the school take account of different cultural and personal naming traditions?[20]

One school, by asking questions like this, soon became aware of the limitations of its policy:

We felt that the collection of information about our children, including information about languages and cultural backgrounds, had been rather hit and miss and that the person collecting the information (the secretary) was not the person most suited to the task . . .[21]

As a first step the staff in this school changed their admission form to include details of children's languages, as well as their religious and dietary needs. Changes also took place in the admission procedure itself:

As most of our children start in the nursery, our admissions are now done by the person with responsibility for the nursery unit. She invites the parents and children into the nursery. She is then able to assist with the form-filling and explain why we need the information. The parents and children can also look round the nursery and ask questions . . . It gives the teachers a chance to form a good relationship with the parents and children and explain the nursery routine.[22]

Having access to someone who can act as an interpreter is important. Sometimes parents will bring along a friend or older child. In some cases the school will be able to call upon the services of a bilingual member of staff, a home/school liaison teacher or a local interpreting service. Whoever is responsible for carrying out admissions and gathering the required information, however, needs to do so with care and sensitivity and be knowledgeable about the varying cultural practices which accompany some of the details that will be requested:

> Certain details need to be collected with particular care and sensitivity because of varying practices across cultures, for example:
> □ Child's date of birth – the system for counting can vary between cultures.
> □ Child's and parents' names – can give rise to confusion when schools are not familiar with naming practices in different cultures.
> □ Diet and eating traditions – are important to know about, so that variations in school meals can be provided if necessary, and so that curriculum work on food can be handled sensitively.
> □ Religion – this information is vital not only so that teachers can understand the background of the child, but so that the parents are given an opportunity to discuss with teachers ways in which their religion is reflected in the work of the school.[23]

Once the child is settled into school the main formal opportunity for continuing contact is likely to be through Parents' Evenings and Open Days. Several studies have shown that parents usually attach considerable value to these as their prime means of keeping themselves informed about their children's development.[24] Asian and West Indian parents are no exception and, as John Rex and Sally Tomlinson demonstrated in the Handsworth survey[25] their record of attendance at such events is as good as that of any other group:

> . . . just over half . . . had been to a parents' evening or open day, which, as most hard-pressed teachers will admit, is not the ideal time to fully discuss a child's progress.[26]

Yet, despite their interest, ethnic minority parents do not always find contact with the teachers a particularly fulfilling experience. Their frustrations have been documented by several writers. Jon Nixon, for example, quoting from the work of the Birmingham-based All Faiths for One Race (AFFOR) group[27] stresses that above all parents want to talk about the education of their children. Unfortunately, the strained formality of parents' evenings is often a barrier to this, exacerbated as it is by lack of privacy, time constraints and a distinct production line atmosphere of receiving set-piece answers to questions. It would be unfair, however, to suggest that teachers themselves are universally satisfied with such procedures. Many are only too aware of parents' frustrations and feel similarly strongly about the issue. Perhaps the time may be ripe to consider alternative ways in which the two groups can be helped to communicate more fully about the children for whom they have a shared interest. One approach, yet to be explored in depth, involves a reversal of the traditional relationship and places the teacher in the listening role.[28] Home visiting, too, has a contribution to make especially if it is imbued with this same 'listening' philosophy. Though traditionally associated with 'problems' and 'crises' and regarded as the responsibility of a designated home/school liaison teacher, the home visiting approach is now coming to be seen by some primary schools as potentially a very effective channel for establishing rapport between home and school and providing parents with opportunity for more sustained discussion with those teachers who are most closely acquainted with their children's development. It is a principle strongly endorsed by the Rampton Committee.[29] Alongside this some primary schools are now firmly committed to encouraging other forms of regular informal contact between parents and teachers: in the playground, at the school gates, in the street or at the local community centre. The value of this type of strategy cannot be overestimated as an aid to parents and teachers becoming better acquainted with each other and, thereby, establishing a relationship of trust and understanding.

Whatever approach is adopted the intention should be to create an atmosphere where parents are able not only to ask questions and seek information but also to express opinions and voice anxieties. Not surprisingly, it is this latter dimension which is likely to pose the greatest challenge to teachers' professional skills.

Parent representatives on the governing body
The 1980 Education Act required that all schools include at least two elected parent representatives on their governing bodies. Only a few years before, Baron and Howell[30] had expressed disquiet at the small number of LEAs that had made any provision for parents, by right, to have their own elected governors. In some areas of the country, therefore, the Act could be seen to mark a major growth in democratizing educational decision making. Yet, as Sally Tomlinson points out,[31] it was a dilution of the recommendations of the Taylor Report, three years previously, that small primary schools should have at least two parent governors and large secondary schools as many as six. In terms of the present discussion, however, the concern should be not only with the actual number of parent-governors but also with the process of ensuring that those parents who traditionally have felt most excluded from the work of the school are given a voice. This is a point stressed by the Rampton Report in its recommendation that governing bodies of multi-ethnic schools should include parents from ethnic minority communities. This immediately raises questions about election procedures. Readers may know from their own experience

that parents are often asked to cast votes in governors' elections without knowing a great deal about the candidates. Even more seriously parents are often not aware of the role and potential power of their governors. Rarely is there any forum for them to receive reports from governors' meetings and, in turn, raise issues which they would like the governors to examine. If addressed, questions of this nature would go some way towards ensuring that the work of governing bodies takes more account of the needs and concerns of parents.

Important as governors are, it would be naive to assume that any single body will be able to provide all parents in an ethnically diverse school with the channels that they need for expressing views and participating in decision making. The need, then, is for a more co-ordinated approach in which governors have a role to play but where a range of other opportunities also exists for dialogue between parents and teachers and collaboration in children's learning.

Parents as helpers on outings and visits
There can be few primary schools where parents are not invited to take part in class outings. Many readers will have had experience of such outings and will be aware of their potential for drawing on the skills and resources of the local community, as well as for acquainting white parents with places and practices associated with other cultures. Visits to mosques, gurdwaras, community centres and food shops have all proved valuable in this respect. It is easy to be sceptical, however, and to argue that working in this way affords only a narrow, even tokenistic, view of parental involvement, that amounts to exploitation of parents, especially mothers, as unpaid teachers' aides. It is becoming quite common to meet parents and community activists who take such a view. That primary schools have been criticized in such terms is a salutary reminder that we are in an age where school/ community accountability is becoming a prominent issue on the educational agenda. Communities are now more questioning about their relationships with schools and they are more likely to inquire about teachers' motives in seeking their support and even to ask what parents themselves stand to gain. This shift from deferential acceptance to sceptical questioning should not be interpreted as a threat to schools. Quite the contrary. For individual teachers it can be a challenging opportunity to reflect more closely on reasons for wishing to involve parents in day-to-day classroom activities. And for the school as a whole it can be a stimulus for examining how small-scale initiatives at classroom level fit into an overall strategy for closer liaison with parents and communities.

Parents working in the classroom

Viewed against the background of an overarching policy of orient-
ating the school towards its community, the involvement of parents in
the work of the classroom takes on a new significance. Of course, such
involvement still has the short-term gain of relieving pressure on the
teacher and allowing provision for a wider variety of activities for the
pupils. Handled with care and sensitivity, however, it can offer many
other benefits such as helping children to relate to a wider circle of
adults, from their own and other ethnic groups; giving parents more
insight into how the primary classroom works; and enabling teachers
to appreciate how parents' skills can extend the work of the class. Let
us take an example. At the present time one of the most common ways
in which bilingual parents are encouraged to contribute to the
classroom is through the use of the mother tongue. One writer[32] has
drawn together (in Figure 3) some of the varied forms which such work
might be expected to take:

PARENTS AND LOCAL COMMUNITIES CAN USE THEIR LANGUAGES TO HELP WITH . . .

Games and rhymes

Teaching games and rhymes to children

Recording rhymes on tape

Craft and cookery

Writing recipes

Cookery sessions with children

Sewing and other crafts

Stories

Telling stories to children

Recording stories on tape

Encouraging children to write mother tongue stories

Music and drama

Helping with dramatic productions

Teaching dance

Recording songs on tape

Teaching songs to children

Translating

Signs, labels and notices

Children's own stories and writing

Books for children

Letters and circulars

Play activities

In the home play area

With sand and water

With constructional toys

Number work

Displays of numbers and counting systems

Counting activities with children

Making games and work cards

Figure 3
HOW PARENTS CAN CONTRIBUTE TO CLASSROOM WORK

Commonplace as some of these activities may seem, for them to become a reality there are a number of difficulties to be overcome. There will be some parents who are unaccustomed to an open and hospitable school regime and it is quite likely that this will give rise to some initial reluctance to accept teachers' invitations to join in. Other parents will have unpleasant memories of school and these may reinforce any other doubts they might have about participation. Also it should not be forgotten that different cultures vary in their perceptions of the role of the school and the teacher/parent relationship. All these factors underline the need for informed sensitivity on the part of the teacher.

The difficulties are not confined to parents. Teachers have a habit of creating professional barriers to home/school collaboration. Many find it difficult to cope with the presence of other adults in the classroom. With other teachers the problem is more to do with threat than inhibition: the presence of non-professionals whose knowledge and expertise in some spheres surpasses their own causes them to feel that their professional competence and standing are being undermined. Barriers of this sort are not easy to overcome. But dismantled they must be if an effective teacher/parent relationship is to develop.

Pre-school involvement
It is a truism to assert that the transition from home to school can be a traumatic experience for parents and children, but when that transition is accompanied by an abrupt switch from one cultural and linguistic world to another the trauma can be heightened considerably. Such has been the concern about the consequences for the child that for some years the transition from home to school has been the driving force behind much of the thinking about home/school collaboration in pre-school education. Initially, the focus was on white working class communities where families, through adhering to life styles, forms of speaking and value systems which differed from those of the school, were thought to be culturally disadvantaged. Thus a major theme in pre-school policies has been to acquaint parents with the cultural norms of the school and to equip them with what were thought to be more appropriate parenting skills.[33] A similar philosophy has been found at work in the pre-school provision for ethnic minority families. Often a major effect of this type of thinking, as Sally Tomlinson[34] points out, has been to undermine parents' confidence in their own parenting abilities by reinforcing a sense of dependence on those 'experts' and 'professionals' whom they perceive as the repositories of all knowledge about 'correct' child rearing procedures. Tomlinson

goes on to argue that this deficit view of ethnic minority and working class parents has far from disappeared. Referring to a number of recent home/school projects focused on the pre-school period[35] she suggests that there is still a tendency for the professionals to make assumptions about parents' needs and expectations or to make a gesture towards consulting parents – only to disregard their views at the stage of implementing ideas. Underlying all this, she argues, is an ethnocentric and often class-biased view of how children should be reared and of the role of parents in the early stages of learning. If we are sincere, then, in wanting to see more effective relationships between parents and professionals at the pre-school phase the starting point should be the recognition that parents, as the recent study by Tizard and Hughes[36] has shown, can be very effective educators of their own children. From this all else should flow. Teachers and nursery staff will have much to gain from observing parents interacting with children and listening to their views about this crucial, that is, pre-school, stage of their children's development. Likewise parents will stand to gain through having the opportunity to articulate their views to others and to draw on the experience of professionals to help them take greater responsibility themselves for the direction and content of education for their young children.

School as a community resource
The concept of 'maximum use of plant' – community groups sharing in the facilities of their local schools – is not a new one: it was a principle underpinning the thinking earlier this century about community colleges.[37] But it was not until the early 1970s, through the work of Eric Midwinter[38] and others associated with the Educational Priority Area projects of the time, that we saw the idea translated into the urban primary school setting. Since then, the concept has gained considerable ground – so much so that it is now not unusual to see schools which have been purposely built, or re-designed, to embody the shared facility principle. In its most common form it means that a community group is encouraged to use the school's facilities after normal school hours. This might take the form of one-off events around festival times or other major occasions in the community's calendars, or it could involve the school becoming a centre for community-run mother tongue classes and supplementary education of the sort discussed earlier. Important as these developments are, however, they will do little in themselves towards fostering closer links between the school and the outside world. No doubt the presence of local people in the school building gives the staff an opportunity to promote their work more widely and, thereby, to break down some of

the barriers to understanding. But if lasting school/community links are to emerge, more systematic work is called for. Houlton and Willey[39] take up this very issue in relation to community mother tongue classes and offer an inventory of suggestions whereby closer dialogue can be established between teachers in community mother tongue schools and the mainstream sector teachers:

1. Links between mainstream teachers and teachers in community mother-tongue schools:
   (a) Following joint teaching themes
   (b) Sharing resources (e.g. use of mother-tongue books in mainstream classes)
   (c) Discussing opportunities for mainstream teachers to support the skills children are developing in community mother-tongue schools
   (d) Providing mutual support for children taking examinations in their mother tongues
   (e) Exchanging knowledge and expertise (e.g. through stories, songs and games)
   (f) Developing joint resources such as packs of teaching materials and stories on tape.

2. Links between mainstream schools and community mother-tongue schools:
   (a) Discussion of teaching aims, methods and materials
   (b) Organization of reciprocal visits
   (c) Exchange of information on individual children and their progress in both schools
   (d) Shared use of teaching resources and facilities (e.g. audiovisual and reprographic equipment)
   (e) Joint in-service training sessions on issues of mutual interest
   (f) Joint activities to celebrate festivals and other community events
   (g) Providing mutual advice (e.g. on the production and purchase of teaching materials)
   (h) Helping mainstream teachers to gain a basic knowledge of their children's mother tongues
   (i) Mainstream schools taking the financial burden of entering pupils for examinations in the mother tongue
   (j) Mainstream schools providing premises for community-run classes.

It was the experience of these two writers that many of the organizers of community mother tongue classes are very enthusiastic about operating in partnership with their mainstream colleagues. Indeed, the suggestions which Houlton and Willey put forward are based firmly on examples of successful practice in the field. They did find, however, that some organizers, whilst wishing to have a rapport with mainstream schools, are not willing for this to be at the expense of their classes' independence. The same theme is developed by Jon Nixon in relation to West Indian supplementary schools. He writes:

Such schools are justifiably proud of their independence from a state education system which many black parents and teachers see as having failed their pupils.[40]

He advises that any relationship between community-run schools and the mainstream system should recognize that the strength of the community's work lies in its independence. It is precisely because these schools are not beholden to the statutory sector that they have the confidence of parents and young people. Nevertheless there is still considerable potential for co-operation of the sort Houlton and Willey suggest, providing that the starting point for dialogue is an open-mindedness on the part of mainstream teachers and a recognition of the achievements of community classes.

Forming a school/community association

Traditionally, school/community associations and PTAs have not been based on the principles outlined above. Usually the impetus for them has come from the school itself and they are seen as serving pragmatic functions such as fund raising for the school and creating opportunities for social contact between parents and teachers. As such they are essentially a white, middle-class concept and, not surprisingly, have had most success in schools where the clientele fit such a description. They have also found some favour in schools serving multi-ethnic neighbourhoods, but here there is a very real issue of conflicting expectations. The school's perception of the association may be firmly within the social-gathering, fund-raising tradition, whereas ethnic minority parents may see it as providing them with a more effective channel of communication with their children's teachers. The conflict between the two perspectives is summed up succinctly in the experience of a black mother from Birmingham:

> Concerning Parent Teacher Groups and meetings – it depends on what the group is like. Some groups actually discuss the children and their problems. Other groups tend to concentrate on raising funds to buy curtains and nonsense like that. I think it's important to discuss the children and how they're getting on because that's the whole point of it. And therefore if your school is one where you're discussing your children's future, then I think it's fine, but otherwise it's a waste of time.[41]

Unfortunately, as Sally Tomlinson perceptively points out:

> Because the aims of PTAs are to encourage consensus and agreement between homes and schools, they rarely incorporate mechanisms for dealing with conflict. Thus, when the interests of parents and schools do not coincide, PTAs may be of little value.[42]

This inability of PTAs to handle conflict, she concludes, might be a key factor in explaining the low level of participation by ethnic minority parents.

What are the alternatives? One might be for the school to foster greater collaboration with those groups who make use of its facilities whilst continuing to encourage more participation by individual parents at classroom level. Another might be for the school to help set up ad hoc organizations in response to specific community needs and interests. One such example, a Mother Tongue Support Group, is described by Twitchin and Demuth:

> The Support Group was set up when a cross-section of people, but particularly those representing the Asian Community, were invited to discuss how the school might respond more sensitively and effectively to the needs of children from Asian homes. It was quite obvious that the overwhelming concern was for the provision of mother-tongue teaching as an extra-curricular activity, or even that it might be included within the school day. After consultation with the LEA, it was agreed that classes could be established, but that they should be for mother-tongue teaching only. It was also agreed that they should be designed to generally assist and enhance the school curriculum, that we should concentrate, at least initially, on the nine to eleven age range and that they should take place after the end of the school day. We were also granted enough money to appoint a co-ordinator on a part-time basis, whose job it was to recruit a group of volunteers who would assist him with the teaching. In no time at all we had classes in Urdu and Punjabi for fifty children. We arranged for them to meet straight after school for an hour twice a week, and although various alternatives have been thought about, this is still the way they are organized. They are extremely popular, and it is clear that we have touched on something that is seen by our parents, and by people in the community generally, as being of vital importance. The Support Group continues to meet regularly and to monitor the progress of the classes. At first it was concerned merely to ensure their continuation. More recently it was agreed to press the LEA for a qualified teacher to be appointed to the school on a full-time basis, who would be primarily concerned with the development of mother-tongue work with very young children.[43]

A further approach might be a school community association of the sort also described by Twitchin and Demuth, only in this particular case the association's brief was to 'protect and nurture' the range of facilities available in the school for use by local people, including 'the playgroup/drop-in centre, the holiday play schemes, the clubs for old people, the various adult activities and the . . . community play area'.[44] The association's independence was protected by its constitution and control of its work was in the hands of a representative grouping of parents, residents, school staff and individuals from voluntary and statutory organizations.

Paramount in both these examples is the notion of partnership. Unlike the more traditional model we see here a coming together of professional workers and local people to identify community needs and concerns and to create bodies which respond to these, but under the control of the people who are most crucially affected. Here, the focus is on an alliance of interests where the school, community and other agencies work together towards commonly agreed ends, rather than on the idea of the school doing things for the community.

Parent education programmes

That modern primary education can be a source of confusion for many parents, especially for those whose own schooling took place in another cultural setting, is often the starting point for parent education programmes. As a rule these will comprise workshops and demonstrations where parents have a chance to become acquainted with materials and techniques which are a regular part of their children's classroom experience but which differ markedly from those in use when they themselves were at school. Hence it is now quite common for parents to be able to attend practical sessions where teachers demonstrate and explain their approaches to teaching reading, mathematics and the use of the computer; the underlying assumption being that informed parents are more likely to be supportive towards the school and better equipped to show interest in their children's classroom work.

Whilst few of us would question the value or desirability of these initiatives they give rise to two sources of anxiety. First, the scenario is a very familiar one of teachers determining what parents should know. Only rarely do parents have the opportunity to articulate their own needs and to collaborate with teachers in working towards meeting them. Thus we see perpetuated a cycle of expert/non-expert, superior/subordinate relationships, with the result that parents are not helped to take control over their own learning, and their own expertise has little room to surface. Second, it is in the nature of these teacher-led programmes that they tend to avoid issues which are potentially controversial, even though these may be high on parents' own agendas. Doubtless, feelings may occasionally run high over the value of, say, using calculators in number work or whether children should be heard to read every day, but usually a full explanation from the teacher will be sufficient to allay fears and restore consensus. Other omissions may be more serious. It would be unusual, for instance, for a parent education programme to include discussion of the school's policy on multicultural education or its proposed mother tongue teaching scheme. Why is this? The explanation must lie, at least in part, in our professional aversion to controversy and our assumption that because certain issues have been a source of disagreement within the profession there is little likelihood of them being harmoniously accepted by parents. Of course, there is some basis to this. Ethnic minority parents are not always unanimously committed to mother tongue teaching, as a teacher reminds us:

> . . . The general feeling among the ethnic minority parents was very strong – they didn't want anything to make their children different. They felt that in England they should read, write and think in English.[45]

And, as Kelvyn Richards reports in his account of an exchange project between two Nottingham primary schools, white indigenous parents may resist even the most tentative moves towards multi-culturalizing their children's learning:

> After the first week the head of the North Nottingham School received complaints from some parents about the project – objecting to their children mixing with 'these immigrants' from the city centre.[46]

The strength of these negative reactions is beyond question, as, too, is the disheartening effect they can have on teachers. Nevertheless schools should be prepared to respond to them, not in a defensive or moralistic manner but, preferably, within a forum that allows for regular and open exchange. It is not inevitable that parents will be hostile to diversity-based learning but where incipient hostility exists we can be sure that it will be aggravated by a closed-door policy on the part of the school. Likewise, such a policy will offer little to those parents who are favourably disposed towards a multicultural curriculum and who would welcome an opportunity of saying so to their peers. What some schools are now moving towards, therefore, is a recasting of the concept of parent education programmes to include the full range of policy and curriculum as well as providing opportunity for listening and learning to become a two-way process, involving not just parents but teachers, too.

Home/school learning programmes
In the same way that teachers can be expected to hold different views about the purpose of parent education programmes, so they are divided in their attitudes towards the involvement of parents in the teaching process. Yet, ironically, most parents are interested in supporting their children's learning and devising a role for themselves which will complement the work of the school. The main barrier to progress, as I have stressed repeatedly, lies in teachers perceiving parental involvement as an infringement of their professional status

and independence. Fortunately, a growing number of primary teachers now feel they can put aside professional inhibitions to respond to parents' enthusiasm and offer them support in understanding the contribution they can make. The most notable developments have been in the area of reading, where there has been no shortage of back-up from authoritative sources. In 1975 the Bullock Report strongly endorsed the principle that parents have a part to play in their children's literacy acquisition. Two years later John and Elizabeth Newson wrote of the 'revolution in literacy' that could be 'sparked off and fuelled by parents and teachers in determined co-operation'.[47] More recently, evidence from schemes in different parts of the country has shown how parental involvement and declared teacher/parent co-operation can significantly enhance children's reading performance.

Among the early experiments were those conducted in Haringey[48] and Rochdale,[49] both of which involved parents from working class and ethnic minority communities. More recent studies have taken place in Coventry[50] and Hackney,[51] again involving parents other than from white middle-class backgrounds. It would be naive to suggest that such schemes have been free from difficulties, both practical and interpersonal, but as more get underway and evidence grows it seems beyond doubt that the benefits to all concerned can be considerable. Perhaps herein we can see a prototype for a new model of parent/teacher relationship – one which can be extended beyond its present focus on literacy to encompass other aspects of language development, together with other dimensions of learning. Certainly such schemes can do much towards equipping parents with sets of skills that traditionally have been seen as the sole preserve of the teacher. Equally they offer us insight into how we might harness the cultural skills, the linguistic knowledge and, indeed, the life experience which parents possess yet which for so long have remained outside the orbit of the school.

Future developments
The questions which inevitably now arise are, 'Where do we go from here?' What is to be the next step in parent/teacher and school/community relationships? Clearly, there are no easy answers: there can be no blueprint for development. Schools vary considerably in terms of what is considered appropriate at any particular stage in the relationship between teachers and parents/community. Even so, from the themes that have emerged so far, there seem to be two obvious next steps. For teachers who have moved beyond the stage of working for the community and now see themselves as working in partnership

with it, one step must be to link up in some way with the community's concerns; in short, to stand with local people on issues that directly affect them and their children. These issues may take several forms: threats to local services, racist attacks or unjust deportations. It is important, however, for teachers to appreciate that though these issues may essentially be outside the world of the school they will profoundly influence children's quality of life and, thereby, their life chances. Thus they are a natural extension of teachers' normal professional concerns. A further step, and one which primary schools increasingly now are trying to take, is to open up decision-making procedures in order to allow for fuller participation by parents. This is easier said than done and it would be naive to disregard the institutional and interpersonal difficulties that lie in the way of setting it up. But, as some are now realizing, it is a logical outcome of the school's becoming accessible to the community and of parents being encouraged to take an active part in their children's education.

Summary
In this chapter we have:
1. drawn upon research evidence to show that working class and ethnic minority parents are as interested as any other parents in their children's education;
2. shown, again with reference to research findings, that ethnic minority parents are frequently dissatisfied with aspects of the education on offer to their children;
3. outlined the reasons for this dissatisfaction as well as the steps that communities are taking, through their own supplementary schools, towards compensating for it;
4. examined some of the components of a co-ordinated policy for home/school relations, touching upon issues such as teacher/parent communication, parental involvement in children's learning and parental participation in decision making;
5. stressed on several occasions that, if the idea of home/school partnership is to become a reality, the relationship should not simply be based on parents being expected to give and to listen; rather, teachers have much to learn from listening to parents but they may need help in order to acquire the skills necessary for them to be able to do this.

Further reading
A comprehensive overview of general issues pertaining to home/

5 Diversity in the classroom

For a school to bring about an 'education for all' of the sort envisaged by the Swann report calls for action at two levels: among class teachers in their classrooms, and throughout the school as a whole in the form of a coherent statement of policy. One without the other will be insufficient. In the remaining two chapters, therefore, there is consideration in some detail as to what this action will entail. We begin by focusing on the classroom since it is there that most of what we are hoping for will be enacted.

Initiatives by individual teachers are in no short supply at the present time and there is much to be said for documenting a cross-section of these to make them available to a wider circle of teachers. After all, one of the main barriers facing teachers is the limited opportunity for their experience to be shared and disseminated. Of course, children's needs vary, not least as a result of the ethnic composition of their schools and neighbourhoods. We cannot assume that strategies which have proved successful in Brixton or Bradford can be transferred intact to classrooms in Bournemouth or Brighton. Nevertheless, the experience of one teacher can do much to inspire ideas elsewhere. And the principles underpinning this experience are likely to be applicable across a range of circumstances. With these points in mind the approach adopted in this chapter is primarily eclectic: it reflects the insights of teachers from a variety of schools. Beyond that, it addresses itself to classroom practicalities by drawing together case studies of classroom experience. And, equally important, it stems from a set of declared curriculum principles which are offered as cornerstones for diversity-based learning, irrespective of children's ethnic backgrounds or the demography of school catchment areas.

The reader will recall the extract from the Berkshire checklist[1] discussed in Chapter 3. I think there is much in it that can inform the present discussion about curriculum change and review in schools. Recall how it suggested a number of topics (for example, diversity, migration, racism) which could form the basis for work in primary schools. It stressed the importance of corridor and classroom displays reflecting the diversity of Britain. It emphasized the need for careful examination and selection of resources. It urged a continuing commitment to challenging racism in schools. And, integral to all this, it outlined an approach to teaching and learning which encourages co-operation among children, opportunity for children to learn from each other and for teachers to learn from their pupils. We find similar themes in a checklist produced by the Inner London Education Authority:[2]

☐ Are issues related to the multi-racial nature of British society today treated in a coherent and comprehensive way throughout the curriculum?

☐ Where there are choices to be made about the content of the curriculum do these take account of the diversity of pupils' cultural experiences?

☐ Is content provided from a wide range of sources? Is it selected so that it engages pupils' feelings as well as giving them information? Are pupils able to explore and share the ideas, opinions and interests which derive from their particular cultural experiences?

☐ Does the curriculum aim to create an understanding of and interest in different environments, societies, systems and cultures across the world?

☐ Are pupils encouraged to recognize that each society has its own values, traditions and styles of everyday living which should be considered in the context of that society, as well as compared with their own?

☐ Are opportunities provided to show the contribution that different societies have made to the growing understanding and knowledge of humankind?

☐ Is the curriculum designed towards developing an understanding and appreciation of the various communities that make up the local and national society?

☐ Does the content of the curriculum ensure that pupils understand that migration and movement of people – and thus cultural diversity – are underlying themes in history and the contemporary world?

☐ Have teachers and departments selected the content of courses to help pupils understand how inaccurate and potentially damaging racial and cultural stereotyping can be, and the historical and contemporary processes which encourage this stereotyping?

Drawing on these two sets of guidelines, as well as principles identified in earlier chapters, we can now compile our own set of curriculum principles which might assist the primary teacher to give classroom meaning to theoretical ideals:

A Classroom Checklist

1. *A Welcoming Ethos*
   Is the general ethos of the classroom welcoming to diversity? Do the teaching and learning styles encourage collaborative working among

children? Is there opportunity for children to voice feelings without threat or risk? Are children able to learn from each other and is the teacher able to learn from them?

2. *A multicultural, multilingual constant*
   Is there a multicultural, multilingual constant throughout the curriculum and the visual environment of the classroom? Is it possible to apply the 'acid test' of entering the classroom when the children have gone home and know from displays, children's work, signs and resources that the teacher has a commitment to cultural diversity?

3. *Valuing children's and parents' experience*
   Do the children and their families feel that what they have to offer is recognised and valued in the classroom? Do they feel confident about bringing their knowledge, skills and experience to the fore and sharing these with others?

4. *Lifting taboos about discussing race and racism*
   Is there a taboo surrounding the discussion of race difference and racism? Do the children feel that these are subjects which are not to be aired in the classroom? Or do they have opportunity to express views and recount experiences? Are the children encouraged to think critically about bias and prejudice in what they see, hear and read?

5. *Learning about and experiencing other cultures*
   Are the children able to learn about and experience cultural systems and styles of living other than their own? Is there opportunity for them to become more fully informed about people from other ethnic groups?

Readers no doubt will wish to extend this list or adjust its emphases according to the priorities in their own daily situations. Nevertheless the list compiled represents some of the more pressing questions facing primary teachers and, as such, is a foundation for a collation of some of the initiatives being taken at the present time. I therefore propose in the rest of this chapter to set out each of the checklist items with examples of practice.

A welcoming ethos

Kalpana is an 11-year-old of East African origin. As part of a discussion about the languages of children in her class she wrote:

> Languages that I speak   Kalpana
>
> I speak gujarati. I can speak gujarati
> very well because I speak gujarati to
> My my mum, dad, and my two sisters.
> I can write a bit of gujarati. Well I
> go to a special school on sundays. I
> have just started about a month ago.
> I can read gujarati quite well but I am
> still learning. My mum can speak other
> languages like punjabi. So can my dad.
> I can count in my language but I can
> only count upto 5 and I am going to
> write it in my language એક
>   બે
>   ૩ ત્રણ
>   ચાર
>   પાંચ.

Alex, a 10-year-old, did not contribute a great deal when her class was
talking about language differences but when the time came to express
her thoughts on paper she wrote (much to her teacher's surprise):

> My Languages.   Alex
>
> I can speak Welsh. I like speaking
> in Welsh. this is how to count to
> twenty.... un, dia, tre, pedwer, pimp,
> llwerdn, sith, uwith, naw, deg, undeg,
> indeodia, irdeg, tre, indegpedwer, indegpimp
> undegnaw, diateg. It is easy to read Welsh
> but not that easy to say it. I can speak
> English as well. Wesh in Wales is cymraeg

In both cases we see children speaking with clarity and honesty about aspects of their cultural and linguistic experience which traditionally have remained concealed from the classroom. That they felt able to share them with others in this way is a tribute both to their own self-confidence and their teacher's success in establishing an atmosphere where differences can be brought to the surface without fear of ridicule or abuse. Yet frequently one meets teachers who present a totally different portrait of their classrooms: pupils deny any knowledge of languages other than English, they insist that their dietary habits do not extend beyond cornflakes and fish-fingers, and they shy away from any discussion about the cultural life of family and community. Attention was drawn to these issues in chapter 2 but at that point little was offered in the way of practical advice for the teacher beyond the familiar exhortation to foster a classroom ethos hospitable to cultural variation. I am acutely aware, though, that phrases like 'a welcoming ethos' and 'hospitality to diversity' have a platitudinous ring unless they are accompanied by an attempt to set out their component elements. They need to be translated, as far as possible, into classroom actuality. Perhaps this can now be done. I have found the following 10-point plan a valuable aid in helping primary teachers understand what is entailed in creating a 'welcoming ethos'.

Towards a welcoming ethos: a 10-point plan for the primary teacher
- ☐ See differences as opportunities for the classroom, rather than as problems to be eradicated.
- ☐ Avoid assumptions that Anglo-Saxon Christian traditions are the norm and that others are deviations from this.
- ☐ Seize opportunities to infuse all aspects of classroom life with cross-cultural perspectives.
- ☐ Encourage all children to bring their out-of-school experiences into class and to discuss these together.
- ☐ Give status in the classroom to all children's cultural knowledge and linguistic skills.
- ☐ Show interest in the children and encourage them to show interest in each other.
- ☐ Respond to race-related incidents as they arise.
- ☐ Show sensitivity to children's feelings.
- ☐ Be aware of your own behaviour in the classroom.
- ☐ Do not be afraid of reversing the traditional pupil/teacher relationship.

There is one theme that underlies each of these points: that is, teaching style. To my mind this is a crucial ingredient for bringing about the type of classroom hoped for. I said earlier that there is no blueprint for managing diversity-based learning. Teachers will wish to evolve approaches according to the circumstances in which they find themselves and in the light of what their experience tells them to be the most effective way of eliciting responses from children. At the same time, however, we can agree on a pedagogic style that should underpin teacher/pupil relations.

Earlier, with the help of Stephen Rowland,[5] I questioned the appropriateness, for diversity-based learning, of the traditional didactic view of teaching, with its image of the teacher as the repository of knowledge and the pupils as the passive receivers of that knowledge. Such a concept of learning would fulfil few, if any, of our 10 points. What, then, are the alternative models? Again we can turn to Stephen Rowland. One model might be the open-ended exploratory technique favoured by many post-Plowden primary practitioners and characterized in the 1978 Primary survey as follows:

> . . . the broad objectives of the work were discussed with the children but then they were put in a position of finding their own solutions.[6]

However, as Rowland points out:

> . . . the idea that learning takes place when individuals are 'put in a position of finding their own solutions' may fail to recognise the essentially social nature of learning. Left on their own during activity, with only their own resources to call upon, students may rely only upon that knowledge and those strategies with which they are familiar. Anyone trying to learn on their own easily becomes stuck into their own ways of thinking. Such ways of thinking may be expressions of a particular ideology of which, on one's own, it is difficult to gain any critical awareness. Without teachers or peers with whom to interact during the process of learning, the student is liable to become more entrenched in her present position. This problem arises whether the subject matter is a mathematical investigation which may require new insights, or a social enquiry which demands a new perspective on issues of racism. The danger is that an exploratory model for learning, while intending to be a radical alternative which empowers the learner with greater autonomy, may actually have the opposite effect by protecting the learner from the challenge of social interaction. Confidence may be gained, but the opportunity for growth lost.[7]

As an alternative he offers the socially-based 'Interpretative Model of Teaching and Learning'.[8] He shows this diagrammatically in Figure 4:

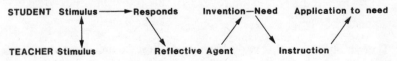

Figure 4
INTERPRETATIVE MODEL OF TEACHING AND LEARNING

For a more detailed explanation of the model we can use Rowlands' own words:

> In this model, the initial stimulus for activity may come from the student or from the teacher. In either case, it is vital that it is the *student's* interpretation of that stimulus which motivates the activity. Only then can the student's control be assured. She is not trying to 'guess what's in the teacher's mind' in responding to the teacher's resources, but formulates her own ideas. Once the activity is under way, the teacher's role is then to act as a reflective agent, aiming to help the student identify concerns and needs, and also to provide positive yet critical feedback to the student. The student, in turn, critically responds to the teacher's contribution. Neither is 'right' or 'wrong'. Both student and teacher are engaged in a two way process of expressing what it is they are trying to formulate and grasping those things which the other person is indicating. In the course of tackling problems, students will invent. Such invention, even where not successful, is a powerful means of increasing awareness of what skills and knowledge are needed. Once the student recognises this need, her control of the activity can be temporarily handed over to the teacher, or indeed to another student, for a period of instruction. This instruction does not have the purpose of developing skills in isolation, but of empowering the student to meet the goals which she has set for herself. In this model, unlike the Didactic model, instruction is an enabler of the student's control rather than a mechanism for concentrating the teacher's control.[9]

For Rowland, the most important implication of the model is that 'the distinction between learners and teachers becomes less clear cut. Learners can become teachers, and teachers become learners'.[10] This notion of teachers becoming learners and, conversely, of learners taking on a teaching role, I am now suggesting should be a fundamental part of the classroom that wishes to respond openly to racism and be genuinely hospitable to difference of culture and language. A particularly apt illustration is to be found among the classroom case studies produced by the Schools Council Project 'Language in the Multicultural Primary Classroom'.[11] Under the title 'Learning from Children', Hilary Hester, the Project Director, writes:

> One of the aims of the Project is to find ways of drawing on children's cultural experiences, and of helping them to share those experiences within the classroom. This is important for two reasons: first, all children need to feel that the personal and community experiences they bring with them to the classroom are valued and understood; second, by sharing their experiences with each other, children can broaden each other's understanding of ideas and ways of living.
>
> One way of finding out what is important for children and what they know about is by talking with them. Sometimes, because our experience is not theirs, it may be hard to follow what they are telling us, because we do

not have the same pictures in our heads. But given an atmosphere they feel comfortable in, children will tell us their experience and knowledge.[12]

She goes on to provide the following extract of a conversation which arose during a discussion, in a history activity, about burial customs.

Telling her teacher about 'burials' in India and Pakistan

Suhail	. . . buries them and they puts . . . um . . . all the dirt on top of them . . . like they put . . .
Teacher	Do they burn them?
Suhail	No, they don't burn them.
Teacher	Who burns them? In which country? Where do they . . .
Suhail	India. India.
Teacher	Come on then, Sanji, tell us about it.
Sanji	Ms . . . Miss, when they are dead, um they um . . . um . . . cut wood and they put the people and they put some more wood . . . top of them, and they burn them.
Teacher	What, do they put them like in a coffin, a wooden box?
Sanji	No not a wooden box.
Suhail	Miss, when children get stabbed in India . . .
Sanji	um . . . um . . . Miss, a piece of this woods they put it under. People put some more woods on top of them.
Teacher	Where, where do they bury them? Where . . . in the street or . . .?
Kuldeep	Inside the house.
Sanji	Not inside the house . . . um . . . um . . .
Teacher	Inside the house?
Kuldeep	Yes, miss. That's where my nana buries and she went right inside the water, right inside the water. My uncle and my other uncles went inside to see her but not little boys.
Suhail	Miss, miss . . .
Sanji	Them's a big boy, is the oldest. If he's the oldest one in the family . . . yeh, yeh, he puts the wood, and he puts more woods on the side and flowers all over it.
Teacher	And they burn it?
Sanji	Yes miss.
Teacher	And they burn it, they burn the body?
Sanji	What
Teacher	They burn the body?
Suhail	Miss, and they burns the face.
Teacher	They burn the whole body?
Suhail	Yes, miss.
Teacher	Do they do this in a graveyard, in a cemetery or in a garden, or where do they do it?
Sanji	Miss, they find . . . do like a park. There's a big place like a park.[13]

It is interesting to notice how the dialogue breaks with the conventional 'Initiation – Response – Feedback' model of classroom discourse[14] whereby the teacher initiates, the pupil responds and the teacher provides feedback. Instead the children take a more active part in determining the content and direction of the discussion. Notice also how the length of the children's contributions is often appreciably greater than the teacher's. Unlike most classroom exchanges the teacher here does not know the answers to the questions she is asking: they are genuine inquiries and thus represent an invitation for the children to take on the teaching role. The children's enthusiasm shows through as they volunteer their knowledge, sometimes disagreeing with each other and the teacher in order to convey accurate technical details. Perhaps the most striking feature of the discussion is the ease with which the children make their contributions: they seem to have no embarrassment at disclosing aspects of their cultural experience, and their trust of the teacher is such that they are happy for her to enter their private worlds. Here then we have a snapshot of a classroom where the teacher has gone a long way towards establishing the required atmosphere.

But lest we should think that the approach advocated is a novel one we should remember that some teachers, especially those who work most closely with nursery and younger infant children, will find little in it which is unfamiliar. After all, in everything suggested here we are still firmly within the tradition of good primary practice, and there is no better way of reminding ourselves of this than by quoting from Carl Rogers' *Freedom to Learn*,[15] especially that section where he compares two 'pathways', two types of primary school experience. The first, I would suggest, is more widespread than we might care to admit. The second sums up the classroom ethos I have in mind when talking about 'good primary practice':

One Pathway to Education

A small boy enters school, his first day. He is eager to go, because it is a step toward being grown up. He knows that big boys go to school. On the other hand, he is frightened. It is a strange new situation, full of fearsome possibilities. He has heard stories about school – about punishments, about exciting times, about report cards, about teachers, friendly and unfriendly. It is a scary uncertainty.

He is directed to his room. His teacher is businesslike. Here is his desk and chair, one in a straight row of desks and chairs. Here are his books, and pencils. The teacher greets the group with a smile but it seems forced. Then come the rules. He cannot leave his seat, even to go to the toilet, without first raising his hand and receiving permission. He is not to whisper or talk to his neighbours. He is to speak only when called upon. No one is to make unnecessary noise.

He thinks of yesterday. He was continually on the move making as much noise as he pleased, shouting to his friends. School is very different.

Then classes begin – the reading books, letters and words on the board. The teacher talks. One child is called upon and is praised for a correct response. He is called on. He makes a mistake. 'Wrong! Who can give Johnny the right answer?' Hands go up, and he is soon corrected. He feels stupid. He leans over to tell his neighbour how he happened to make the mistake. He is reprimanded for talking. The teacher comes and stands by his seat to make clear that she is watching him, that he must abide by the rules.

Recess is fun – much shouting, running, some games – all too short.

Then the ordeal begins again. His body squirms, his mind wanders. Finally lunch. Not until they are all lined up in a perfectly straight row are they permitted to walk, silently, to the lunch room.

His educational career has commenced. He has already learned a great deal, though he could not put it into words.

He has learned that:

☐ there is no place for his restless physical energy in the school room;
☐ one conforms or takes the unpleasant consequences;
☐ submission to rules is very important;
☐ making a mistake is very bad;
☐ the punishment for a mistake is humiliation;
☐ spontaneous interest does not belong in school;
☐ teacher and disciplinarian are synonymous;
☐ school is, on the whole, an unpleasant experience.

At the end of the day, he asks his parents, 'How long do I have to go?' Gradually, he will learn that he has been sentenced to a very long term.

As the days, months, years roll by he learns other things. He learns that:

☐ most textbooks are boring;
☐ it is not safe to differ with a teacher;
☐ there are many ways to get by without studying;
☐ it is okay to cheat;
☐ daydreams and fantasy can make the day pass more quickly;
☐ to study hard and get good grades is behaviour scorned by one's peers;
☐ most of the learning relevant to his life takes place outside of school;
☐ original ideas have no place in school;
☐ exams and grades are the most important aspects of education;
☐ most teachers are, in class, impersonal and boring.

A Second Way to Learning

A small girl goes to school for the first time. The atmosphere is friendly and informal. Part of her fear and anxiety disappear as the teacher greets her warmly and introduces her to some of the other children.

When it is time for school to begin, they sit in a circle with the teacher. She asks the children to tell of one thing they are interested in, one thing they like to do. The teacher's interest in each youngster is evident, and the little girl relaxes even more. This may be fun.

There are all kinds of interesting things in the room – books, maps, pictures, building blocks, crayons and paper, some toys – and soon the children are investigating their environment. Our small girl looks at a picture book of children in another country.

When the teacher calls them together again, she asks the girl if she could tell a little story. Our youngster starts to tell about going shopping with her mother.

The teacher prints part of the story on the board and points out the words and letters. And so the day has begun.

What has this small girl learned? She has learned that:
☐ her curiosity is welcomed and prized;
☐ the teacher is friendly and caring;
☐ she can learn new things, both on her own and with the teacher's help;
☐ there is room for spontaneity here;
☐ she can contribute to the group learning;
☐ she is valued as a person;

We don't need to follow her school career further because it has all been described in earlier chapters. But in this humanistically oriented school, we will find various elements as she continues through the years.
☐ She will have a part in choosing what she wishes and needs to learn.
☐ She will learn reading and mathematics more rapidly than her friends in other schools.
☐ She will find an outlet for her creativity.
☐ She will become more expressive of both feelings and thoughts.
☐ She will develop a confidence in, and a liking for herself.
☐ She will discover that learning is fun.
☐ She will look forward to going to school.
☐ She will like and respect her teachers and be liked and respected in turn.
☐ She will find a place in school for all of her many and expanding interests.
☐ She will develop a knowledge of resources, ways of finding out what she wants to know.
☐ She will read about, think about, and discuss the crucial social issues of her time.
☐ She will find some things very difficult to learn, requiring effort, concentration and self-discipline.
☐ She will find such learning very rewarding.
☐ She learns to attack tasks cooperatively, working with others to achieve a goal.
☐ She is on the way to becoming an educated person, one who is learning how to learn.

A multicultural, multilingual constant

Figure 5 overleaf was drawn up by a group of infant teachers as a summary of the steps they have taken towards permeating their curricula with a reflection of cultural and linguistic variety. For convenience the teachers chose to focus on those aspects of the

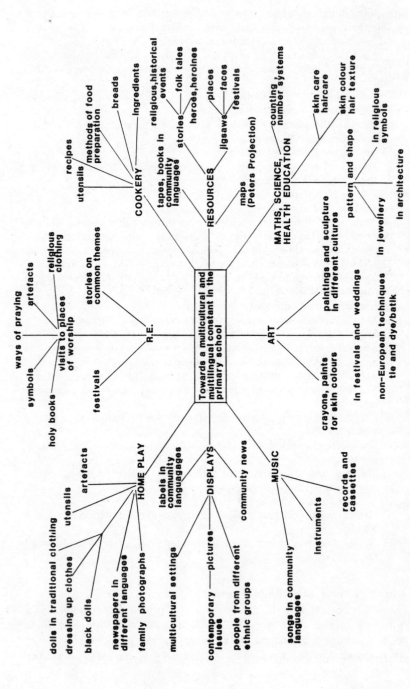

Figure 5 A MULTICULTURAL CURRICULUM FOR THE PRIMARY SCHOOL

curriculum which assume most significance in their classrooms. They would stress, however, that they do not conceive of the curriculum as a collection of separate subjects each with its own discrete body of knowledge. The reality of their classrooms is very different and is based more on the concept of integration between different curriculum areas around a common set of skills and concepts.

The themes incorporated into the chart fit in well with good primary practice and are not identifiable solely with children of ethnic minority backgrounds. Also, and this is a point which many primary teachers would stress, although the themes may stem from an overt recognition of cultural differences, each can sit comfortably within normal classroom activities. Thus we begin to see how the permeation ideal might take effect.

To add more detail to this essentially sketchy outline we turn now to some of the examples of practice which have been documented in recent years.

Valerie Glass was concerned about the essentially white European ethos of the Home Play area of her infant classroom. She set about transforming this to reflect more accurately the cultural worlds of her pupils:

> In providing a Wendy House or Home Corner, we are giving children opportunities for development of language, imagination and social inter-action in role-playing situations. However, it is essential to provide the appropriate resources, which must include things familiar to children if they are to make full use of them.
>
> Asian children require many things not usually provided in this area. Perhaps this list will help not only teachers of Asian children but also motivate those of mainly white classes to examine more closely the resources they are providing, whether their children are from urban or rural backgrounds.
> - Asian clothes – trousers, saris, scarves, sandals, etc.
> - jewellery.
> - greeting cards at religious festivals, Eid, Diwali.
> - candles, plasticine Lamps at Diwali.
> - calendars, pictures showing Hindu gods.
> - chapatti board and rolling pin.
> - saucepan for making tea.
> - Asian newspapers, magazines, filmposters.
> - Asian dolls.
> - material to use as saris.
> - Asian sweets.
> - tapes of Asian film music.
> Children can enter into a play situation more easily when they are using

materials they would find in their own home, instead of those which a teacher thinks they should use!

In a Leicester Infants school, a Punjabi mother was invited to show photographs of her daughter's wedding and discuss it in Punjabi with a small group of children. This gave them the opportunity to use their first language in school in a more formal situation, thereby showing that the school respects this despite its apparent preference for English as the communication medium. It also resulted in Asian wedding scenes in the Wendy House, with children improvising by using curtains to cover the floor to resemble the gurdwara (church). They gave toy coins and paper flowers to the couple and wrapped a story book in a piece of cloth for the Granth Sahib (Holy Book). At last a more exciting role for the boys – guru instead of dad! The introduction of a Punjabi Primer resulted in Indian school scenes, with a row of children copying the alphabet under the close supervision of a 5 year old teacher!

We need not limit the Wendy house to such banal activities as tea parties and housework. A variety of resources means a variety of interpretations – it may be a temple one day, a cinema the next. Teachers of mainly white classes can adopt similar methods if they consider the life style of their children. They can begin to prepare them for life in a multiracial society by introducing dolls and photographs of people from various ethnic groups into everyday activities in the classroom, so that some degree of familiarity and acceptance may be established at an early age.

Cultural differences [*eg* use of different utensils in cooking and eating] should be encouraged rather than corrected if children are to feel confident in establishing their identity outside the security of the home.[16]

The model she describes is now far more commonplace in infant and nursery classrooms, especially those that serve multicultural neighbourhoods, but even so it is not unusual to visit some which mirror the world of a Janet and John reading scheme rather than the contemporary Britain in which children are living.

In the field of 'multicultural mathematics' one of the pioneer contributors has been Ray Hemmings. In an article in the NAME journal[17] he makes a number of suggestions to show how a primary school's mathematics programme can be enriched by drawing on the counting systems and design traditions of other cultures. He writes, for instance, of the value of children listening to counting in different languages, comparing the sounds with those that they know, listening to the rhythm of counting and noting differences and similarities between one system and another. He stresses the importance of children learning something of the history of mathematics, especially of the debt which Western Europe owes to Arabian mathematics for providing the basis of our present system of symbols and computation. And in a final section of the article, using examples of children's work, he looks at the different forms of geometrical art which are found in the

Rangoli patterns used by Hindu and Sikh families to decorate their homes on important occasions, and also in the design and decor of Islamic buildings.

The theme of Music is taken up by Norah Woollard, a teacher in Reading:

> One way in which the whole school shares an interest in language variation is through music. The school meets together once a week for singing and music-making, using songs and music from a variety of cultural traditions. Songs with simple repetitive lines in different languages feature regularly. An overhead projector provides words and outline drawings for clues to comprehension. Actions, of course, add a dimension of enjoyment and give meaning . . .
>
> Future plans for the music session include small group workshops making instruments in traditional folk style and finding songs in languages to match with the help of parents and friends of the school.
>
> Given the right encouragement bilingual children will themselves be able to contribute musically. Panjabi-speaking children have brought tapes of film music from home. Listening to the songs in small groups naturally stimulates talk about the films in which they feature, and the livelier the discussion the more likely it is to take place in Panjabi. In a mixed age group this can mean older children explaining the plot, action, relationships and characters to younger ones, and in a mixed language group Panjabi-speaking children can develop their skills of translation in an atmosphere of keen enjoyment. We have recorded children singing film songs as well as collecting soundtracks. We have played them while doing jigsaws or drawing, and interestingly, children who have not freely used their mother tongue in school, began to insert Panjabi words into their conversation about the jigsaws and their drawings.
>
> A natural outcome of the children recording their own songs was one child volunteering his mother, who came to spend some time in the nursery and recorded songs and nursery rhymes in Gujarati.[18]

In describing a method of working that clearly has been very successful and has enriched the curriculum in many ways, Norah Woollard does not shy away from some of the difficulties that have arisen. She talks frankly about the difficulties that can arise when some children display hostility to other languages, difficulties that are not necessarily confined to music activities or language-based work. Her comments are included here not to introduce a negative note to the discussion – after all much of the debate about cultural diversity in education has tended to focus on the problems and difficulties rather than the opportunities and challenges – but to show how one school has responded to an issue which elsewhere could deter progress:

> We have had occasions when music from different cultural traditions has prompted embarrassment or ridicule, and given rise to stereotyped

Figure 6 PLANNING A TOPIC

HARVEST
an example of a recurring school theme which can enable recognition of linguistic and cultural diversity

The school library
1 Tape recordings of 'harvest stories' in different languages.
2 Class books on display, including cookery books.
3 Displays of food.
4 Pictures of harvests from a wide variety of countries.
5 A good book selection on harvest themes from all over the world.
6 Finding out tasks displayed in library.

Display work, signs and posters
1 Use of photographs to depict harvest produce.
2 Harvest displays in different languages, perhaps some translations made by older children in the school.
3 Fruit and vegetable paintings together with real examples, named in different languages.
4 Food alphabets.

Science
1 Soil.
2 Agricultural methods and crops world-wide.
3 Climate.
4 Nutritional aspects of food in different environments.
5 Cycle – Steiner's rotting apple.
6 Introducing 'own' harvest – growing of alfalfa/mustard/ sunflower seeds.
7 Seed dispersal.
8 Soil/water experiments.
9 Progression of growth from a seed to the kitchen shelf.
10 Food labels as a starting point for finding out about food from different countries.
11 Collection of harvest fruits and nuts.
12 Planting bulbs.
13 Different types of food storage world-wide.

Games
1 Oranges and lemons.
2 Co-operative version of 'Hot Potato'
3 A 'Feely-Box'.
4 Dingle-Dangle.
5 Oats and beans.
6 Cumulative shopping games.
7 Apple bobbing.
8 Finger games.
9 Games of different cultural origins evolved from harvest celebrations.
10 Guessing games.
11 Conkers.

Maths activities
1 Symmetry and shape of fruit and vegetables.
2 Fractions.
3 Graphs of different food consumption patterns.
4 Sorting – leading to matrices.
5 Counting of fruits and seeds in different languages.

Cookery
1 Visit a mill.
2 Use flour to make breads of different cultural origins; chapattis, bread, pizza, buckwheat pancakes, etc.
3 Visit the market.
4 Visit an allotment.
5 Use of vegetables, fruits, nuts, fish and staples to cook dishes of a variety of cultural origins.
6 Involvement of parents with cooking of different dishes.
7 Taking a series of photos in the sequence of cooking one item and then making into a dual text book.

Writing
1 Develop the value of sharing through a class book – extend into poetry and 'harvest theme' books.
2 Translate class books into different languages and make transliterations.
3 Make use of examples of packaging and advertising.
4 Make use of food labels in different languages.

Music-making
1 Instrument-making using gourds and dried seeds.
2 Harvest songs and dances from different cultural traditions. e.g., Panjabi harvesting songs and dances from the Indian subcontinent.
3 Thanksgiving songs generally.
4 Sharing songs.
5 Creating music to simulate weather, farm machinery, animals, etc.
6 Creating music to accompany harvest stories.
7 The use of related themes through movement.

Art and craft
1 Vegetable printing.
2 Natural dyeing/batik.
3 Collage using seeds.
4 Corn dollies and harvest craft traditions in other countries.
5 Colours, named in different languages.

caricaturing. Reactions of children can be noted and, we feel, should be dealt with (usually more effectively) in the smaller class groups. Classroom work can relate to the themes and images of the music to validate it, and by making cultural and language variety a constant, and so a natural part of the classroom, we are working to overcome negative reactions.[19]

Most primary teachers are likely to turn to topic work to help in infusing classroom practice with cultural and linguistic variety. For some the approach has been consciously to select topics that conveniently lend themselves to permeation. Others have preferred to explore diversity as part of a theme which is already under way with the class. From a pedagogic point of view this latter approach may possibly be more taxing since it means not only that teachers have to be aware of the cultural potential of a topic but also that they are able to pursue this with children in such a way as to maintain a balance between their multicultural objectives and other learning purposes. The need for careful planning therefore assumes considerable importance. Figure 6 shows how a group of Berkshire teachers approached a 'harvest' topic with a permeation principle in mind.[20]

We can immediately see how these teachers have tried skilfully to ensure a balance between all the normal primary school activities, while providing opportunities for children to contribute their own experience and at the same time participate in the cultural knowledge of others. Yet despite the prominent position which topic work occupies in the primary classroom there are few teachers who feel confident to plan a topic beyond describing the key 'content' areas with which it will be concerned. Thus there is a pressing need for guidance on planning procedures. I therefore wish to conclude this section by offering a model for planning classroom topic work.[21]

The unadorned model, Figure 7, is set out below:

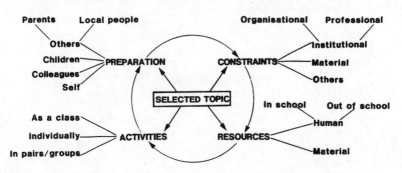

Figure 7
A MODEL FOR PLANNING CLASSROOM TOPIC WORK

The model identifies four interrelated elements which should figure strongly in a teacher's planning. These are, *preparation* of self, colleagues, children and others; likely *constraints*, of an institutional nature, of material shortages, etc.; *human and material resources* available to support the work; and finally the *activities* which children might undertake. The lists below show how two Junior school teachers utilized the model in order to help them prepare for a topic on Number Systems.

A Topic on Number Systems

Preparation

of self:
. preparing collection of project materials (books, charts, other resources)
. personal research into number and counting systems.

of children:
. preliminary discussion about the topic
. asking for contributions from home (e.g. calendars from different cultures, different sorts of money)

of parents:
. informing them about the work to be done
. asking for their help in specific areas

of local people:
. contact with shopkeepers, library, post office, bank, in preparation for visits

Constraints

organisational:
. shortage of adults to help with trips etc.

professional:
. possible resistance from colleagues at the divergence from standard practice
. limitations of own knowledge/ experience

institutional:
. difficulties of getting access to bilingual expertise
. lack of interest of other members of staff

others:
. possible hostility from some parents

Activities

as a class:
. skipping rhymes, number rhymes in different languages
. yard games, counting in different languages
. different alphabets and number systems
. birthdays, calendars, time telling in different cultures

as individuals:
. making individual calendars
. sums in different languages
. abacus work

Resources

human – in school:
. maths specialist

human – out of school:
. adults who can count in different languages
. children themselves
. Language Centre staff

material:
. examples of different numerals
. tape recordings of counting/ number rhymes in different languages

. counting in different bases
. books about particular numbers
. using different scripts
in pairs and groups:
. sorting numbers
. matching work
. domino games with different number systems
. cuisenaire rods
. board games from different cultures
. measuring/weighing – units of measurement

Valuing children's and parents' experience

Traditionally, teachers have been led to see themselves as the repositories of all knowledge in the classroom and to believe that learning can only take place on their initiative and under their direct control. It takes courage for teachers to break out of this way of thinking and to recognize that there are many aspects of life for which their own backgrounds have ill-prepared them. Even greater professional courage is called for if they are to admit that there are many of their pupils who have knowledge and skills which in certain matters far surpass their own. Fortunately many primary teachers are now creating within the classroom learning contexts that enable children and their families to bring their skills to the fore as resources for all to share. Some examples of how this is happening are set out below.

At Alexandra Infant School in Haringey, parents, teachers, children and many others connected with the school came together to produce a small booklet called *Spinning Tops from Around the World*. In her introduction, Elizabeth Singleton, a teacher at the school, describes the approach they used:

> The contributors of this book about spinning tops are all connected in some way with Alexandra Infant School in Wood Green in Haringey. Some of the children, parents and grandparents have written on the theme. They were joined by the caretaker, the cleaning lady, a dinner supervisor, an educational advisor, the head teacher, one of the meals staff, a teacher and her brother in law, and the welfare assistant's husband. They range in age from five to seventy three. The adult contributors look back to childhoods spent in eleven countries, and have written in eight languages.[22]

The following pages contain numerous examples of writing, much of it autobiographical:

From Lancashire.
Whips and tops - in 1930's.
In the little corner shops, crammed with licorice sticks, monkey nuts, ½d sherbet dabs, and lucky bags - there we would find tops. At ½d each would be the mushroom shaped ones or at 1d the coloured green or blue ones. Children would have to decide whether they could afford to spend their Saturday penny (or ha'penny) on a top, instead of sweets. Whip and top season would be when the weather was dry and the ground on the waste areas was firm. The school playground or street were the best places to play. In those days there were very few cars - only carts pulled by horses, belonging to the milkman or baker, would stop your play. How I envied the boys who could crack their whips and make the tops spin gaily up and down the streets, making the tops hop up and down the kerbs or over other obstacles. All too soon the top season was over - time next to play with 'jacks'.
                                                    E.M.Clucas.

When my mum was small she used to play with a top and whip. They call it "Toupie et Frelequet" She didn't have to buy it then, her big brother would make one with a firm piece of wood. It was played on the ground. The way she did it; roll the whip around the top and the one who makes it spin most is the winner.
                Naden Chinasamy. Mauritius.

My Daddy used to Play with the top in Egypt. He was very good at it.
Mona Morsi

One is immediately struck by the genuine community participation. Here is a school drawing to the fullest extent on the linguistic and cultural resources of its families and neighbourhood. In viewing its community as a resource the school is giving status and validity to the knowledge and skills that the community possesses. Thus it is doing much towards fostering relationships with the world beyond the school gates and at the same time helping the members of that world towards a greater awareness of themselves.

Teachers elsewhere have taken up the same principle in relation to other themes. Subash Sachdeva, a Leicester teacher, involved his class in collecting examples of games played by their families. He writes:

Fortunately I know quite a few games myself having played them as a child. I was able to learn more through my class children. They were asked to talk to their parents and relations and find out from them the sorts of games they had played when they were young. After gathering information the children who understood the games well were asked to explain to other children in English, Gujarati, Punjabi and Kutchi. I also brought in video films, like 'Naseeb' and 'Chota-bhai' where college students are shown playing Kabadhi and other games.

KABADI

This game is a test for your breath and strength. You have to teams. you could call them team A and team B. there should be equall teams. then the two teams get behind their boundary. The one person comes for Team A and stands on the starting point and them he or she says Kabadi, Dabadi or aaaaa and as they are saying that he or she have to tick team B without he or she running out of breath. If he or she stop saying Kabadi Kabadi or aaaa . . . then they quickly run back to there team if he/or she runs slowly then one person for Team B can tick the person that is going back. If he or she gets ticked then the children he or she had ticked is not out. He or she is out because they got ticked. Then you have turns ticking each others team until they are all out. In India they play another one which is very rough. You have to trip the people over or pick them up and get them away from the line. so when he or she stops saying Kabadi Kabadi or aaaaa they can get ticked.

Rupa

KING ASHOKA

This game is usually rouf, usually boys play it but girls can play it. One person is in the middle and all the other people are on one side. And the people who are out on the side has to say
  Har Har Mahadeve
and the person in the middle says
  Naam Ashoka
and then All the people on the side has to run through the middle and the person in the middle has to catch as many people as he can and he has to hold onto them until everybody's gone through. All the people he has cort has to be on with him and they then all do the same until one person is left and then that person is named
  KING ASHOKA

Minaxi 23

My class then played these games for the rest of the school and the children and teachers were given the chance to ask questions. My children wrote about the games in different languages and also added some art work. We followed this up by inviting another class to join us in our P.E./ Games period.

It is valuable that these games require no special equipment; the children and their parents are the resource and they can be enjoyed during playtime and dinner break.[23]

Other aspects of a family's experience may be more charged with emotion. Many families will have poignant memories of migration and teachers may wish to draw upon these as part of classroom work. For primary teachers, however, a problem arises in deciding how to approach such a theme in a way that is appropriate to pupils. Studying topics of this nature can so easily become little more than sterile exercises in information transmission and regurgitation which have little relevance to children's lives. If these difficulties are to be avoided the strategy in the primary school should be both practical and participatory and should utilize the experience gained by pupils and their families. In multicultural classrooms there is an immediate link with the theme through the children themselves. Nowadays, far fewer children of primary age have first hand experience of migration, for the vast majority will have been born in Britain. Nevertheless, almost without exception, ethnic minority children will live in families where migration has left among parents, older siblings and grandparents enduring memories of war, political upheaval and economic uncertainty. And almost inevitably there will be vivid recollections of the period of arrival in Britain and the prevailing climate among the 'host' population. It is important to remember, though, that migration has not been confined to black or ethnic minority families. Many white indigenous families, indeed whole communities, have their own experience of migration as a consequence of unemployment and economic hardship which drove them to search for work elsewhere. There is therefore scope for interpreting the theme in a non-exclusive way that relates directly to the events in many families' lives.

The following shows how one teacher introduced the subject of migration with a primary class. Using the idea of a simulated radio programme, Mike Slack asked children in the class to play the part of their own parents being interviewed about their experiences in coming to Britain. Here is an extract from the 'programme' with a child interviewer talking with different members of the class:[24]

Interviewer: What was your first impression of London?
Child: I was very shocked . . . there were many houses on top of each other but in Trinidad there was plenty of space.

I didn't like it much because there was too much smoke. In St Lucia there was no smoke at all because we didn't have many cars there.

I didn't know what winter was at first because of the snow . . . I just got confused.

Interviewer: Was it difficult to get West Indian food?

Child: It was really difficult because they didn't import it at that time so we had to eat English food which I didn't like much.

Interviewer: How did people react when you first came to this country?

Child: Well, they were staring at me in a peculiar way and they threw stones through our windows.

Interviewer: Did you ever encounter any prejudice?

Child: Once when I was going shopping these skinheads come and said, 'Go back to the jungle where you come from.' And they started throwing stones at us and I just hated it.

Interviewer: What were your neighbours like when you first came?

Child: They were friendly to us and if, like, we never have something we would go and ask them.

From here Mike Slack went on to encourage discussion about the children's everyday experience of racist incidents:

M.S.: Has anybody got any bad experiences they would like to tell us about? Yes, Namisha.

Child: In my other school I was the only coloured person and the children there used to call me black African and lots of other bad words.

M.S.: Has anybody else had any similar experiences to Namisha?

Child: Well, when I first came to this country people called us names and they said that we came from Africa when we came from Jamaica.

Child: When me and my friend were playing we went past this lady's garden and she come out and said 'don't come near my garden, go back to the jungle where you belong'.

The same migration theme has been explored by a Berkshire teacher, Linda Cushine, with her class of Third and Fourth year juniors. Reproduced below is her account of the work as it appeared in a local publication, *Looking into Language*:[25]

'After hearing some Anansi stories, the idea for our project came from the children themselves', writes Linda Cushine, whose class of third and fourth year juniors traced Anansi's people from their African roots to America and the islands of the Caribbean and so to new black experience in Britain.

We began by going back 300 years to a time of long-standing stability in many African countries and examined the laws and social support of rural communities. We saw how young people were educated within the community and how history, politics and sociology were included in the oral tradition of story-telling.

We talked about how and why story-telling and the Anansi tradition continued to develop during life on the plantations.

We considered life on a plantation, the various kinds of work that would have to be done, the splitting up of families, the climate of the Caribbean. Would the West African people recognise any of the plants and animals? How did the Creoles of individual islands evolve? How much were the languages affected by various conquerors – Dutch, French, Spanish and British planters?

We listened to stories told by people from different islands – with different accents, different dialects. Children of Bajan origin compared the way their parents spoke with the stronger dialect of their grandparents. One of our teachers comes from Guyana; she discussed various words which are limited to isolated areas. A boy whose family originates in Azad Kashmir in Northern Pakistan talked about his own interest on listening to children from other areas of Pakistan who speak Panjabi, but in a different dialect.

What had become of Anansi's people who stayed in Africa? The children copied the Zulu Song of Freedom and its English translation. We talked about apartheid and its effects on family life. How would we feel? I tried to make it clear that there had been black people living in Britain for many, many years and that there had been establised black communities in Liverpool, Bristol and London since the seventeenth century.

What brought people to Britain? How did their expectations compare with what they actually experienced? One black child quoted her father, a resident in Britain for many years: 'In wartime you're white, but when the peace comes, you're black again'.

Then came the slave-traders and the forced removal of many thousands of people. The children were most concerned by the appalling circumstances in which people were thrown together. They were from many different language groups. The children asked: 'How did they communicate?' 'Were they frightened when they did not know where they were going?' 'If they were all young people, how did they cope without the support and authority of their elders?'

We examined the place of initiation ceremonies for young people and came to the conclusion that there are many parallels in our society today.

With the ending of slavery in America we looked at the life of Harriet Tubman and her work in the aftermath of the Civil War – how she attempted to ease the passage of hundreds of ex-slaves in their expectation of a life of freedom in the industrial northern states.

Children asked their parents what had brought them (or their grandparents) to live in Reading. We found our families originated in Eire, Wales, Scotland, Italy, India, Pakistan, Tunisia, Barbados, St Vincent and Grenada.

I talked about my own grandparents whose poverty drove them from the Orkney Islands which had been their family home for hundreds of years.

At this point in our project, I felt the children were more prepared to talk about the prejudices they and their families still experienced. One black child who had reacted very negatively to our earlier talk about Africa was able to say just a little about names he's been called and how he 'didn't have to put up with it'.

For Linda Cushine the initial impetus for discussing migration came through story material, but the topic progressed in such a way that before long she was able to give a central place to the children themselves and their families. Both case studies illustrate well the child-centred principle which I have stressed repeatedly. Readers should appreciate, however, that an approach of this sort depends for its success above all on the teacher's ability to establish a relationship of trust and understanding where both children and parents feel that their personal experience is welcome and can be discussed without fear of hostility or ridicule.

Published materials can be helpful but, to state a truism, they can at best only complement the teacher's own efforts. Unfortunately there is little that has been published related to this field. Perhaps the most notable example is the Children's Language Project,[26] a pack of activity cards designed to help bring the study of diversity more prominently on to the classroom agenda. One card from the series deals directly with questions of migration and movement of people. It takes as its centre-piece a world map showing how the family of Yi-Ping, a seven-year-old Cantonese speaker born in Glasgow, has migrated around the world. After reading and discussing details of the family, children using the card are set a number of tasks:

> Find out if your own language has travelled to different parts of the world. Do you have any relatives who live in other places? What are their names, where do they live and which language(s) do they speak? You could make your own map like Yi-Ping. Or you might like to do one with your friends to show where your relatives live and which dialects or languages they speak.
>
> You could also talk to people you know about the places where their relatives live and about the languages they speak there.

There is much scope for children to carry out research into their own families and enlist family members as resources for learning. Like some of the other approaches shown, this may have its initial focus in an ethnic minority experience but the principle of non-exclusiveness means that discussion is broadened so as to tease out elements which are common to the experience of all.

Lifting taboos about discussing race and racism
We talked in Chapter 2 about how children from an early age are aware of, and curious about, race differences. Evidence was also shown that from a similarly early age children may internalize the prevailing message of our society that it is good to be white and inferior to be black. At that stage, however, we said little about the steps that primary teachers can take towards helping children develop a more balanced view of race differences and to respond critically to racism

when they encounter it. I would therefore like to offer some examples of how teachers who, having recognized the degree to which race and racism are part of their pupils' daily experience, have set about responding in a manner consistent with good primary practice.

Martin Francis, like Mike Slack whose work we discussed earlier, is another teacher who appeared in the BBC-TV programme, 'A Primary Response'.[27] In the programme we see him at work with his class of Third and Fourth year Juniors at Normand Park School in Fulham. Before discussing his method of working it might be helpful to read his rationale for bringing race-related questions to the fore in the classroom. The following is extracted from an interview with him on the film:

What do you say to people who accuse you of foisting political issues on young minds?
Well I'm only following the ILEA policy – it's called a multi-ethnic policy – which fully recognises the dangers of racism and what it does to school children. At this moment in our borough the young National Front has been leafletting schools and claims they are getting very good support from white youth. There are marches, racist graffiti, and news of violence. So it is an issue for the children anyway. What I'm doing is lifting the lid off it so that through discussion they can discover what racism is and what has resulted from it before. I think it would be a 'political' act to ignore racism – to pretend that everything's fine when, as the children themselves have already realised, it's not.

But aren't these children a bit young to discuss such an issue properly?
Because racism is part of their daily experience they can never be too young. I know a nursery school teacher who takes up racial issues with parents who've told her their own children are not to play with black children, for example. It has come through from nursery to primary school, and if we leave these questions to secondary school, during the adolescent phase, when they may have fears about not getting jobs and so on, this can leave them ready prey for those racist groups leafletting outside the school.

If we tackle this in primary school, it perhaps won't be set aside later in just a special social studies class, for example. As a primary teacher, I have the children all day, and if an incident occurs, I can stop the lesson, get the children around, and talk about it on the basis of a relationship built up over a whole year. With mutual confidence, they talk about the way name calling really affects them, for example. This is not so easy in secondary school where it's harder to have a special relationship with one teacher. The vital thing is to respect their feelings, because all the time I'm encouraging them to reflect that what they say counts.

What then do you say to a child who has apparently very racist feelings?
If a child makes racist comments, or gets involved in a fight with a racist undertone to it, we talk it over in a discussion circle. I get the whole class to

talk about it – and that way it's often the other children who deal with the racism. When they talk about their own experience, this can get through to the child better than me. After all, the peer group live in the same streets and experience the same sorts of things. But the difference, between what a black child experiences in terms of harassment, and a white one, is important. And it's important that the white children learn what this difference can mean. I think in our discussion this is what comes out. Similarly, I stimulate their understanding of what it feels like to be in a group that is scapegoated, through study with the children of *The Diary of Anne Frank*. The children can identify with the emotion of someone who was herself a child at the time of writing; and to show that oppression can be resisted, we talk through the revolt of the black students in Soweto, who are attempting to get a better education system.[28]

Notice how, when something racist arises among the children, his response is not censorious or prescriptive. Rather, he gives the class an opportunity to 'talk it over in a discussion circle', where each child has opportunity to speak when a stone is passed to them. We join the class during a discussion about racism in the neighbourhood:

M.F.: I want to hear about your experiences of that, what you feel about it and what you think can be done about it.

Child: Sometimes when black people walk through alleyways, the NF walk by and start beating them up.

Child: If someone calls someone else a name then I think the person who was called the name should go to the head and the other person should be made to say what they had against the person or why they said it.

Child: Well, I'm black but I'm still English 'cos I come from this country, and when they say 'get back to your own country', I just say in my mind 'well, I come from this country so I can't go back nowhere'.

Child: I think people who call Indian people pakis are a bit stupid because how do they know they come from Pakistan?

Child: . . . some people call me paki but I'm not because I come from East Africa.

Child: I think they should stop the Ku Klux Klan and NF and just make friends . . . just because they're black, probably they're just the same . . . just the same body or something but just in a different colour.

Here we see how race issues can be handled openly in the classroom in an atmosphere which is not charged with high emotions and where the simple expedient of passing a stone ensures that every child has an opportunity to speak and that others are expected to listen. Such an approach, of course, calls for a trusting relationship between teacher and children and needs to be complemented by continuing provision for cultural diversity throughout the curriculum.

Perhaps one of the most widespread manifestations of racism among children is in name calling, jokes and taunts. This is just as common in 'all-white' schools as in schools with significant numbers of black or other ethnic minority children, but it is rare to find teachers anywhere who feel confident about tackling it. Some persist in denying its existence altogether, or turning a convenient deaf ear to incidents as they arise. Others will excuse the behaviour on the grounds that the children 'don't mean it' or 'don't understand what they're saying'. Many, however, are acutely aware of the problem but are unsure about what their response should be. One teacher's starting point, with a class of 10- and 11-year-olds, came during follow-up activities to a programme in the ITV 'Tomorrow's People' Series.[29] Her strategy was the now familiar one of bringing children's own feelings and experience to the fore, in this case with a view to producing a class book, *Sticks and Stones*. She writes:[30]

Immediately after the programme, the whole class gathered together. The class teacher and I (I am a specialist teacher for English as a Second Language) talked about names we had been called. She is completely deaf in one ear, and I am very tall, so we both had stories to tell.

The children responded very well to our honesty and to the intimacy of the situation, and all but one talked readily about name-calling they'd experienced. In this particular class, one child is slightly spastic, another has a bone disease and uses crutches. Several others have characteristics which they are very self-conscious about so not all the names were racist, as they had been in the programme we had just watched.

We talked about the different situations that give rise to name calling, and the differences between nicknames which are offensive, and those which are affectionate.

Name calling

When people call me names it usually hurts sometimes but when people call me nick name's like chubby cheeks I dont mind because I know that they are only Joking but when Im called names like halfcast I feel very sad. When I'm at home my sister calls me Fatty but I don't mind.

When I am out in the playground
some people call me,
KELLY BAKES CAKES!
And I feel very sad,
They say that I am stupid
because my mum is Irish,
and they make *trouble* on me.
When I am at home
my dad calls me,
DOGS,
cause sometimes my name is in the

paper
on the dogs races
and the horses,
I don't think much about that
because my dad is only joking
and he don't call me horrible names.

Inevitably, once the children were in an atmosphere where they could talk frankly and openly, discussion turned to racist name-calling. The teacher set out her rationale in this way:

Racist name-calling by children connects with racialism in society as a whole – with discrimination and disadvantage in employment and housing, for example – in a way that wearing glasses and being called 'four eyes' doesn't, and approaching name-calling in this way raises serious questions. For instance, would some now take advantage of their friends' feelings and use names known to hurt, during confrontations? This worried me, but I myself feel the approach is justified, for children *need* to discuss any characteristics *they feel* may put them at a disadvantage. They also need to understand what it's like to be on the receiving end of verbal abuse. Therefore, it seemed to me the best way to do this was to call on the children's experience of, and feelings about, being called names.

Name calling

One day at brownys I was called black nigre and I didnt like it. I dont like being called that becoause I will get up set. Then I hit her and then we started a fight and in brownys you are not alud to fight and I was very hurt.

When I was in the infants
they were not calling me names,
But when I got into the juniors
they started calling me names like
handicapped
and blacky,
I do not like it at all,
I do not call them names,
Why do they pick on me?
I do not pick on them.

Few teachers, of course, would think that an exercise of this nature could in itself bring an end to the more abusive forms of name-calling among children, and this particular teacher does not make any lofty claims for the work's lasting effect. As a result of the issue being handled in an honest yet sensitive manner, however, she found that the children became far more considerate of each other's feelings and certainly more reticent about using names which they knew to be hurtful. Perhaps this is justification enough for the work she did.

Learning about and experiencing other cultures

Everything I have said so far in this chapter is as applicable to all-white or white majority schools as those serving multicultural neighbourhoods. In white majority classrooms the case for exploring questions of racism among the children is as compelling as elsewhere. It is equally important for cultural diversity to be recognized and established as a constant across the curriculum. And the relationship between the styles of learning fostered by the teacher and the creation of an atmosphere that is welcoming to variation of culture, language and ethnicity is just as strong. One would hope, therefore, that teachers of ethnic majority children would accept this continuity of purpose and move on to translate principle into practice with whatever modification of detail and emphasis is needed. Unfortunately some teachers continue to think it is necessary to devise strategies specifically to suit those classrooms where homogeneity rather than diversity is more the norm.

Perhaps, then, some space should be given to explore some of the curricular approaches that teachers are taking in such situations.

By far the most common approach is the 'getting together' idea – the organization of direct person-to-person contact between children from schools in city centre multicultural neighbourhoods and others from more suburban, predominantly white, areas. A variation on the theme is to bring contact about on a 'distance learning' basis, through the use of pen pal or tape exchange schemes.[31] Either way, the assumption is that by making opportunity for closer inter-ethnic contact at a one-to-one level ethnic majority children will become both better informed about the cultures of others and less susceptible to racist influences.

One of the earliest such initiatives of which there is any detailed record took place in Leicester in 1975 and involved a series of visits between East Park Primary School, where the vast majority of children were of East African, Gujarati-speaking background, and Cort Crescent, a Junior school on a city-fringe council estate. In *Getting Together,*[32] the booklet which records the work, the teachers set out their rationale as follows:

> Some time prior to the project, we had become aware within our own schools of two major sources of concern for teachers. These were firstly the attitude of indigenous children towards minority group children and adults (particularly Asian). The second source of concern was the attitude of the minority group towards themselves and their own culture. We were concerned at the incidence of self-rejection among these children. This seemed to manifest itself in various ways in the classroom such as embarrassment at being reminded of their families' origins and reluctance to discuss aspects of their culture in the presence of children from outside their immediate culture.

We concluded that since our two schools were so different from each other – one all indigenous and one predominantly Asian – a project based on a series of reciprocal visits between the two might provide opportunities for approaching these questions with children.

In drawing attention to these two considerations – the growth of racist feelings among white children and the apparent self-rejection of ethnic minority children – these teachers speak for others who have undertaken similar ventures in subsequent years.[33]

The project involved five visits in which the two sets of children participated in a variety of activities, including workshops on aspects of Asian culture, picnics, kite flying, swimming and other joint events. Afterwards, the Cort Crescent children were encouraged to record their thoughts on paper:

My mum and dad keep saying lots of things about Indian people. My dad calls them golliwogs. But I say, 'you don't know them because you have never met them. They are ordinary people like us but they are coloured'.

At first I thought they would be wearing saris all the time and they would speak in Indian languages but I was wrong. They only wear saris on special occasions. They were human just like us. Because their skins are a different colour doesn't mean to say they are different all together.

My mam said she don't like them and I said 'how do you know, you haven't even met them. I have made a friend there and his name is Dilip'. When my mam says all those nasty words I thought that it was cruel because they are only human like us, only they eat different food.

Pleasing as these responses are, however, the teachers felt it important to retain a touch of realism in their conclusions:

Clearly one can easily make the mistake of over-emphasising the importance of children's ideas as expressed through their writings, by interpreting these as indicators of significant changes. This is tantamount to self-deception. Nevertheless, we feel that this writing, for many of the children, marks a step forward from the views expressed prior to the project, in the direction of developing greater respect for other people and their way of life.

They were similarly restrained in the conclusions they drew about the Asian children's response. The success of the whole venture was such, however, that they were able to feel justified in claiming some achievement and in being optimistic about the value of the work they had done:

As for the Asian children in the other school, it would be foolish to over-emphasise the significance of observations alone, but we have become aware of some encouraging developments. The most important of these, and this has been commented upon by many members of staff, is the greater willingness on the part of the children to discuss themselves, their backgrounds and elements of Indian religious and cultural life with which they are familiar. They are more likely to talk freely about their festivals, their visits to the temple and the weddings which they attend. The shyness which overcame them in the past whenever such matters were raised is no longer in evidence. Perhaps we have made a modest move towards achieving the objects which we outlined at the outset of the project.

An account of a similar project is provided by David Fitch,[34] a Bradford teacher:

> . . . a group of teachers from Bradford LEA and Humberside LEA met for a three-day conference to discuss a pilot scheme of visits between four schools from the two authorities and hopefully to encourage a growth in the number of schools involved. It was reported, by an education adviser from, as he put it 'the white hinterland of Humberside', that the idea of multicultural education had not originally been perceived as an issue to be taken seriously in his area, but that there was a growing awareness that teachers especially in all-white schools, in all-white areas should be helped to make the education they provide relevant to the wider British and world situation. 'Our white children need to come into contact with the real world outside.'
>
> By means of exchanging photographs, tape-slide programmes and even video tapes children had been able to introduce themselves, and during the next few months there were further exchanges of writing, pictures, topic work etc. with the pilot project culminating in a 'demand' from the children involved that they should be given the opportunity to meet one another. This was arranged last summer and some of the spirit of the meetings was captured on video tape.

As in the Leicester example we are given a flavour of the white children's comments, only this time there are 'before and after' comparisons:

BEFORE
They've only got black skins to protect them from the sun.
Is the sun hot in Bradford?
It must be, silly? They've still got black faces.

AFTER
Yesterday Sharon and I sat on the school wall and waited for the Bradford children to come . . . The first thing I noticed were the excited children peering through the windows . . . we all got on the bus and went to the beach . . . some of the girls wore saris, they were beautiful . . . the Bradford children had brought food for us to try, like samosa, kebab, pakora, yellow rice and chapati. The samosa was very hot . . . after dinner we were meant to build sand castles but we went looking for crabs instead, they are started coming out of the muddy sand so I went back . . . later it was time to go and we shouted goodbye, waved and got off after a lovely day.

The Fitch article is also helpful in raising some important discussion points about 'linking' arrangements of this sort. Quoting Bochner[35] he points out the dangers of assuming that interpersonal contact will in itself reduce tension and anxiety between different ethnic groups:

> . . . contrary to popular belief, inter-group contact does not necessarily reduce inter-group tension, prejudice and discriminatory behaviour. Yet one often hears politicians, church leaders and other public figures saying that if only people of diverse cultural backgrounds could be brought into contact with each other, they would develop a mutual appreciation of their points of view and grow to understand, respect and like each other.

The evidence, he argues, in fact seems to suggest that inter-group contact may sometimes have the reverse effect to that which is intended: it may actually increase the hostility and suspicion which is meant to be eradicated. Again with reference to research findings, he offers some valuable practical advice on the factors which seem to be most influential in reducing prejudice. Teachers hoping to embark on similar schemes, he suggests, would be advised to heed:

☐ equal status of the participating groups;
☐ close rather than casual or superficial relations;
☐ contact situations involving interdependent activities;
☐ inter-group co-operation;
☐ contact situations that are pleasant and rewarding;
☐ a lack of competition between the groups.[36]

Jean Adams is a nursery teacher in rural Cumbria who is also acutely aware of how such a geographical location can have a restricting effect on children's horizons. She writes:[37]

> It's very unusual for children to see someone of different race or colour in our district. We occasionally see Chinese, Japanese and possibly Ugandan Asians in Carlisle but not very often. Since some children are often left at home during shopping trips into towns, the chances of them seeing a black face, except on the television screen, are virtually nil.

In order to help overcome this 'deficiency' in the children's world she provides a range of resources reflecting ethnic and cultural variation:

> . . . we have both black and white dolls in our home play equipment and a selection of story books such as Ezra Jack Keats *Whistle for Willie* and *Snowy Day* (Bodley Head 1966–67). Great favourites at the moment are Joan Solomon's books about Berron and Montrice, and Kate Leah's about children in a mixed racial community.

She hopes these resources will go some way towards helping the children to accept as natural the presence of people with skin colours and styles of living different from those which they know. However, she is quick to point out that these vicarious experiences are no substitute for direct contact with people:

> . . . stories and pictures are not the same as seeing and mixing with adults and children of different cultures. So we welcome visitors of different race or colour to come to see us . . . Over the past few years we've been fortunate in being able to encourage a number of adult visitors from a variety of ethnic groups. Teachers have been able to visit and work with the project – three from Japan, others from the New Hebrides, Zululand, Netherlands, America, Kenya – so that our children have not been totally dependent on television and book representation of people from other cultures.

Living in an isolated community the children, as one might expect, are inclined to be withdrawn with people who are new and unfamiliar to them. Their 'first reaction . . . to the visitor, any visitor, is to stare. Some even shrink away and won't sit next to the visitor for a while'. But this withdrawal and shying away is all the stronger when the visitor is of a different ethnic background, and it is usually at this point that the children's misconceptions about race begin to surface. One mother said: '. . . he really thinks the colour will wash off like make-up'. It is this race naivety on the part of the children, as well as their inclination to make evaluations of people on the basis of ethnic and cultural differences, which make Jean Adams all the more convinced of the importance of what she is doing:

> In twenty years or less, our nursery children of today will be parents themselves. Some will carry on the traditions of farming in the same place as their ancestors before them. Some will undoubtedly travel further afield into different social and educational spheres. But whether they remain or go, I feel that even before they reach the age of five, it is important that the foundations be laid for future attitudes and relationships with people of other cultures.

For my final example I shall take another predominantly white community, this time on the outskirts of urban Nottingham. Westdale Junior school serves the middle class suburb of Mapperley. Over the years it has had very few black or other minority group children. Indeed one's impression on visiting the school is of an overriding ethnic homogeneity, in stark contrast with schools situated slightly nearer to the city centre. As with other similar schools the impetus for establishing a diversity-based element in the Westdale curriculum came from one individual, who then involved other members of staff. In this case the individual was Jim Green, the deputy head. He writes:

> On making the move . . . from an inner city multi-ethnic primary school to an all white junior school in one of Nottingham's more desirable suburbs, I

was keen to introduce a multicultural element to the curriculum . . . my initial efforts were confined simply to my own classroom and were quite low key. However, the response from children and parents was positive, and this led to an . . . across-school one term venture . . .[38]

The approach taken was influenced by several considerations. In particular, the staff were anxious to safeguard against the danger of seeing initiatives in cultural diversity as something 'extra' to the curriculum. They therefore set out to establish a multicultural strand within the mainstream of their classroom topic work.

Their 'venture' took the form of a topic entitled 'How we live', inspiration for which came from '*Man in Place, Time and Society, 8– 13*',[39] a Schools Council Project which provides teachers with a model for planning thematic work in the classroom. Briefly, the model proposes a method of working that involves identifying the objectives, skills, personal qualities and key concepts that might be pursued as part of any given topic. Using this approach, the Westdale staff, together with their pupils, set out to examine a variety of social issues in relation to the key concepts: similarity, differences, values, beliefs and power. Integral to this examination was a series of visits and exchanges involving the children and staff of Windley, a multicultural primary school near the City Centre.

The plan that follows, taken from a teacher's booklet developed at Westdale, summarizes some of the preliminary thinking that took place.

'*How we live . . .*'

Key concepts:

Power	(e.g. Why do we have rules? Who makes decisions in school/home/country?)
Values and beliefs	(e.g. How do we live in our community? Why do we live this way? Why do people live where they do?)
Similarity/ difference	(e.g. How is Windley different from our school, home life, food, pastimes, festivals?)

Skills:

Intellectual	Communicating through appropriate medium
	Interpreting pictures, etc.
	Evaluating information
Social	Awareness of significant groups
	Understanding of how individuals relate to such groups
Physical	Manipulate equipment to find and communicate information
	Ability to explore expressive powers of human body, to communicate ideas and feelings
Personal	Fostering of curiosity through questioning
	Exploring personal attitudes and values

Table 5. 'How we live' resource grid

Skills	Power	Values/beliefs	Similarity/difference	Activities
Intellectual				
Communicate through appropriate medium.	World power		Census returns – (library); pre-Windley visit; visit to inner-city school.	Making map and graphs of ethnic groupings; video and tape from school visit.
Interpret pictures etc.	Census returns	Religious practice; ethnic artefacts.	Diet – computer programme.	Survey (24 hours); comparative – inner city school child; evaluate results – computer programme; examination and investigation.
Evaluating information.	Family photos; world power (East/West Third World)	Reference material available.	Diet–menus, shops.	School library ref. book investigations; TV programme 'Custom Made'; exchange visit to include area; photo and video; houses, shops; lifestyle reflections; cultural comparison; historical perspective via photos; interviews – grandparents.
Social				
Awareness of significant groups within community.	Family groupings; school decision-making system; role of government.	Religious practices; ghettoes.	Stereotype game; comparison schools (with inner city).	Questionnaire – comparison inner city school; analyse and compute results; role play – simulations;
Develop understanding of how individuals relate to such groups.	Family groups; rules, laws; world power; (East/West Third World); resources v. population.	Marriages; sex roles; family life.	Comparative weddings; family life.	watch and discuss 'One of the Family' TV programme – (West Indian family); examination of power structure (teachers, parents, governors, L.E.A., central government); school rules; need for laws and law making process; look at government; group presentation (haves and have nots); simulation (East/West Third World); Defence expenditure v. Third World needs); visit a Gurdwara.

Physical Manipulating equipment to find and communicate information.		Religious practices.	Pre-Windley visit; census returns; Windley visit; diet – computer programme.	Produce *Newsheet*; video; TV programme 'Watch'; festivals.
Ability to explore expressive powers of human body to communicate ideas and feelings.	Family life	Comparative weddings.		Role play and simulation 'An Asian Wedding' TV programme; 'Indian Weddings' TV programme.
Interests, attitudes and values Fostering curiosity through encouragement of questioning.	Rules, laws	Beliefs and customs; religious practices, e.g. 5K's, Sikhism, ethnic artefacts.	Comparison of schools.	Reporting back following research into.
Exploring personal attitudes and values and relating to other peoples.	Prejudices – history	Sex roles	Rural and inner city lifestyle.	TV programme; watch and discuss; colour and sex roles; role play.

Possible content:

Family	Family groupings: nuclear, extended, peer groups, marriage.
Food	Diet, health.
Religious beliefs	Prejudices, stereotypes.
Political systems	Structure, history – school, housing – city centre, suburb, villages etc.

Some specific concepts:

That family structures and lifestyles are to some degree 'forced' by necessities of social situation

Assumptions about the way we expect members of any ethnic group to behave

What values support these beliefs?

In what ways is family life different/same in different cultures?

How different is reality from our assumptions . . .

The teachers then went on to prepare a resource grid as a further aid to planning and monitoring the topic (see Table 5). This is very much a working document produced by the teachers for their own use but it provides a useful picture of the breadth and variety of the work that was undertaken during the course of one term and, just as importantly, it shows how the various elements fit into a cohesive whole.

This chart, which summarizes one group of teachers' early attempt to shift their practice in a diversity-based direction, serves as a fitting conclusion to our review of classroom experience. In it are illustrated several of the themes which this chapter has set out to examine. Extending children's horizons beyond their immediate cultural worlds towards the cultures of the wider community; providing direct experience of other cultural forms and the people who live them; recognizing the contrasts as well as the inherent similarities between different life-styles; raising questions about children's personal attitudes and assumptions in relation to people of other ethnic groups: these all featured in the teachers' programme. So, too, did the need to reflect the wider world and political context in which children are living. In addition, and these are not recorded on the chart, the teachers found it necessary to consider a number of other questions, all of which influenced the effectiveness of their work. How, for instance, can primary teachers acquaint children with other cultural forms at a level beyond the superficial and the exotic? How, pedagogically, can teachers draw on elements of other cultures in a way that has meaning and relevance to children in all-white communities? And what materials are available to ensure the necessary accuracy and depth in resource back-up? Perhaps the chart's main contribution is to underscore one simple point, that whatever approach is adopted it should take place within the context of the mainstream curriculum and employ methods that are consistent with the best tradition of primary practice.

All this calls for a broad-based and carefully planned strategy. Although the individual teacher can achieve a great deal, his or her work can expect only limited success if it lacks the structural support of a school policy. In the final chapter I would therefore like to consider in some detail the issues entailed in bringing such a policy to fruition at the primary phase. But first to summarize the main points that have emerged from this chapter's overview of curriculum responses.

Summary
In this chapter we have:
1. discussed existing checklists for reviewing the classroom curriculum and prepared a set of guiding principles for primary teachers, both those in schools serving multicultural neighbourhoods and those in areas with few ethnic minority children;
2. extended these principles with examples of classroom practice drawn from different age groups and different types of schools;
3. urged that, in order to create a classroom atmosphere which is hospitable to examining questions of diversity, race and racism, teachers should try to break with the traditional didactic teaching style and allow more opportunity for children's own views and experiences to come to the surface;
4. advised that curriculum change should not be approached on an ad hoc basis but within a framework of infusing all aspects of classroom life with a multicultural and multilingual dimension;
5. demonstrated something of the range of accomplishments that reside among children and their families and shown how these can be incorporated into the work of the class in a way that is appropriate to all children and not just those from ethnic minority backgrounds;
6. reaffirmed the degree to which awareness of race and racism figures in children's lives and considered ways in which teachers can recognize this in the classroom;
7. reviewed some of the strategies most commonly used by teachers in predominantly white schools, whilst reiterating that such schools should not consider themselves as having discrete needs;
8. maintained throughout that in reorientating their curriculum emphases teachers should not suspend their normal judgement about what constitutes good primary practice.

Further reading

Helpful checklists for reviewing classroom practice are contained in a number of LEA policy statements, in particular Berkshire County Council (1983) *Education for Racial Equality: policy paper 2: 'Implications'*, and ILEA (1981), *Education in a Multi-Ethnic Society – an aide-memoire for the Inspectorate*. The publication which best sums up the teaching style advocated in this chapter is Rowland, S. (1984) *The Enquiring Classroom*, Falmer Press. For a valuable compendium of classroom approaches see 'A Primary Response', programme 2 in the BBC-TV series, *Case Studies in Multicultural Education*. This series, however, has little to say about World Studies in the primary classroom. Readers might therefore wish to consult Fisher, S. and Hicks, D. (1985) *World Studies 8–13: A Teachers' Handbook*, Oliver and Boyd.

6 Towards a school policy

In previous chapters I have attempted to set out some of the main dimensions to the discussion of cultural diversity in the primary school. This began with a context-setting first chapter in which the nature of diversity in Britain was discussed and the responses at school level reviewed. In subsequent chapters some of the emerging issues were considered from the perspectives of children, and parents and communities. Each chapter highlighted some implications for classroom practice which were then drawn together for closer examination in Chapter 5. I prefaced that chapter, however, by stressing the need for classroom initiatives to be viewed in the wider context of a school policy. It seems fitting that this final chapter should return to that theme to set out just what might be entailed in devising such a policy and putting it into practice.

Starting points

Schools will have their own reasons for deciding to set their classroom initiatives into a broader policy framework. Some will be doing so as a result of a directive from their LEA. In Leicestershire, for instance, each school's governing body has been asked to consider a report on multicultural education prepared by the head and it is intended that this report should 'form the basis of a whole-school policy to be developed by staff and governors'.[1] In addition, each school is now required to prepare a statement on racism for inclusion in the brochure issued to parents, 'thus publicly expressing a commitment to education for racial justice'.[2]

The Swann report, too, takes up the question of school policies and its recommendations will doubtless provide further impetus for school-based initiatives. Referring to the Secretary of State's national review of the school curriculum and his request for schools to set out their own curriculum policies, it says:

> . . . we would wish to see all schools including some reference in their policy statements to the need to reflect today's multiracial society throughout their work . . .[3]

The report therefore recommends that 'All LEAs should expect their schools to produce clear policy statements on "Education for All" and monitor their practical implementation'.[4] The theme is further developed in relation to questions of racism in schools, with a recognition of 'the need for schools to develop explicit policies to combat racism':

> . . . all schools must accept their reponsibility for helping to counter the overall climate of racism by adopting a clear stance against it.[5]

But some schools, irrespective of their LEAs' requirements and recommendations from official reports, have taken action under their own volition.In Holloway School in North London, this was brought about when organized racism in the form of a National Front leaflet intruded into the life of the school. As a result the headteacher, George Spinoza, felt impelled to draft a statement for a staff meeting. It began:

> The discovery of this leaflet makes it necessary to have a school policy on the subject to enable us to deal with possible problems in the future. At the same time we must be careful not to over-react. It is true to say that the racial harmony in the school is far better than in most London schools and that the staff are united in their opposition to all forms of racialism and racist ideas. However, we must not be complacent. Racialism outside schools is becoming gradually more respectable and this development will inevitably have repercussions inside schools.[6]

Other teachers have seen a professional and moral responsibility for themselves in breaking down the isolation of the school from the world outside and the issues which children in urban, multi-ethnic communities daily face. Mike Mulvaney, an infants school head, expresses it this way:

> It is tempting, and easy, to withdraw into the school and use it as a fortress against a hostile environment. It is possible to make the school comfortable, warm, and beautiful. We can use textiles and teasels, stuffed owls and soft lighting, double mounting to really magnificent effect. We can isolate our schools completely until they look as though they had been lifted directly from rural Lincolnshire, Berkshire, or Oxfordshire. We can even have an anti-racist policy that operates fairly effectively in the school. However, we only have the children for six to seven hours a day. The rest of the time they must function within the environment that we successfully shut out or disregard.[7]

A further group of teachers would describe their recognition of the need for a policy as indicative of having reached a particular stage of awareness. This was the case at Childeric School in South London. The headteacher, David Milman, writes:

Our growing awareness led us to examine our curriculum provision. It was becoming obvious that what we were engaged upon was an enterprise that affected the whole life of the school as well as the curriculum. We realised that multi-ethnic education was not a new subject on the curriculum to be timetabled among the humanities – rather there was a need for us to examine all of our practices with the multicultural dimension in mind.

We grew to feel the need for some sort of statement of our aims and beliefs. Our discussion had also led us to become more aware of racism – both the institutional racism inherent in any Eurocentric primary school and racism in our pupils and the wider community. It was clear that we would also need some sort of policy and a sensitive uniformity of approach in combating this racism.[8]

Whatever the school's reasons for embarking on a policy statement there is a remarkable degree of consensus over the benefits that can accrue. We can summarize these as follows:

A policy statement provides:
- [ ] a means of affirming to children that the school values all cultures and languages equally;
- [ ] a public declaration of the school's commitment to equality and justice;
- [ ] a source of guidance and support for teachers;
- [ ] a corporate view of the goals of the school and how to achieve them;
- [ ] a basis for appraising the school's progress towards its goals;
- [ ] a means of bringing coherence and continuity to children's learning;
- [ ] a means of ensuring that racist incidents are dealt with seriously;
- [ ] a way of gaining the confidence of ethnic minority communities.

The process

I have stressed on a number of occasions that curriculum change and development in schools involves not only thinking about the *what*, – the content – of teaching but, equally important, *why* that content has been selected and *how* it will be enacted with children. I wish to preface discussion about the content of school policies by considering the process of policy formulation. Unfortunately this is an aspect of the debate which is frequently overlooked, even by those LEAs which are currently requesting policy responses from their schools. There seems to be an assumption that headteachers will know not only what should be included in a policy but also the steps to follow in order to compile it.

There are exceptions and the Inner London Education Authority is one of them. In its 'Anti-racist guidelines for ILEA establishments', the authority offers the following advice:

> Most of the schools and colleges that have developed policies have found it essential to follow a process which includes all of the following:
>
> 1. Placing the issue firmly on the school/college agenda and making time for discussion and development.
>
> 2. Coming to grips with what racism is and its historical context.
>
> 3. Considering how racism can and does operate in the school/college's particular circumstances.
>
> 4. Analysing both directly conscious racist behaviour and what the Rampton Interim Report terms 'unconscious racism'.
>
> 5. Analysing both individual behaviour and the policies and practices of the school/college.
>
> 6. Analysing the behaviour and practices of individuals and services that impinge on the life of the school/college.
>
> 7. Drawing upon the advice and experience of others, including other schools/colleges and those with specialist knowledge and experience.[9]

Schools will certainly find these suggestions helpful as they embark on their own policy formulation, but they may be extended further.

There are several questions to be considered:

Who should be involved in planning a policy?
Traditionally in primary schools, policies on curriculum and other aspects of school life have been drawn up by the headteacher usually (but not always) in conjunction with the deputy head and the holders of appropriate posts of responsibility. But as management training becomes more widely available to primary heads, and more schools begin to attach greater importance to staff participation in decision making, this 'top-down' model of curriculum change is gradually being called into question. Objections can be raised to it on several counts, not the least of which is that if curriculum innovation is to have meaning for teachers, they should be involved with it not just as passive recipients but as participants in its creation. Patrick Whitaker, in his advice to primary heads, takes up the theme as follows:

> . . . members of organisations more readily support decisions they have had a share in making.[10]

He goes on:

> . . . there is likely to be an improvement in the quality of decisions made if all those involved in the life of the school have the opportunity to

participate in solving problems relevant to them. If there is a genuine desire to share power and also to accept the responsibility that goes with it, decision-making can become a positive and dynamic force in the school, not only increasing the job satisfaction of all those involved, but helping to raise the level of identification of individual needs with those of the school as a whole.[11]

This is a principle which we now see being applied with greater regularity across the range of school-based innovation and it is no less valid in relation to policies that have at their heart a more responsive approach to cultural diversity: a point recognized by the NUT in its evidence to the Swann committee:

In the Union's view the most effective way to implement a multicultural curriculum will be through consultation and discussion involving all members of staff of a school so they can work out together an effective policy and strategy based on local needs and resources available to the school.[12]

We see similar sentiments being voiced by the Swann report itself:

It is essential that if any meaningful progress is to be made in bringing about the reorientation of the curriculum along the lines we have suggested, individual teachers are actively involved . . . in reviewing and, where necessary, revising their own work.[13]

The report goes on to warn that if changes in policy are 'simply dictated from above', without any process of consultation, teachers are not only less likely to feel commitment to implementing the changes being proposed but they may interpret their exclusion from decision making as a slur on their professional competence.[14]

What are the methods of working?
If we endorse the principle that teachers should be able to claim a policy as their own and feel confident that it reflects their concerns and priorities, we need to consider how their participation in the decision-making process might be facilitated. There are probably two most frequently used approaches. In larger schools detailed planning work may be handled through a working party. Ideally this should comprise a representative grouping of staff and not just those who already have a strong commitment to multicultural education. In smaller schools the exercise could be undertaken by the staff as a whole, with the option of breaking down into smaller groupings when appropriate. Let us now develop these ideas further. Larger primary schools have much to learn from the experience of those secondary schools which have already been through a policy planning exercise. Peter Mitchell describes the process that was followed at Quinton Kynaston School in

North London, and in so doing he offers valuable advice to those primary schools where size dictates a working party model:

> For a number of years we have made decisions on all major school policies at full staff meetings. Establishing the school's policy on racism has thus followed the same procedure . . .
>
> Each year we decide on major areas of concern which need to be reviewed. The subjects chosen are then posted in the staff common room so that any member of staff may join the Working Party. The group then meet on average five times per term.
>
> Before making recommendations on school policy, a Working Party will normally report to staff meetings so that staff are kept in touch with how their findings are developing. This was a particularly important part of the development of the school's policy on racism . . . through their reports to staff meetings they were able to make the whole staff aware of the issues involved in such a sensitive part of school life . . .
>
> This pattern of work gave an immediate legitimacy to the deliberations of the Multi-Ethnic Working Party, and helped reinforce the idea that the commitment of all staff is needed if a policy on racism is to have any significant influence on school life.[15]

There are some points to be underlined here. First, the notion of accountability: although the working party is charged with responsibility for drawing up the policy, it is accountable for its decisions to staff meetings. So at no stage are staff allowed to feel that they have abrogated responsibility to others. Second, it is likely that belonging to a working party of this sort will be a growth experience for the individuals concerned and will lead to a raising of personal awareness about multicultural education.[16] It becomes all the more important, then, that the working party should not lose touch with the rest of the staff and that its members should be able to explain and defend their decisions to other colleagues whose awareness and commitment may be at a different stage of development. Finally, by ensuring that discussion and report-back sessions involve the whole staff one is also helping to ensure that the policy development process takes on an in-service education role.

Smaller schools might have much to learn from the experience of the Nottingham primary school described by Janet Atkin and Kelvyn Richards.[17] This school had evolved a multicultural emphasis in several areas of work:

> . . . multicultural displays and topics were common; Eid, Diwali, Chinese New Year, and other festivals were celebrated; the purchasing of multi-cultural and mother-tongue books was seen as important; mother-tongue was occasionally in use in the classroom and some teachers were attempting to learn Punjabi. There had been some involvement of parents in school sharing aspects of their life style, and an International Evening and efforts

to help parents with the problems of the Nationality Act.[18]

This stage had been reached not by conscious planning but largely 'through the awareness of the Headteacher, and through the efforts of the ESL teachers to stimulate staff interest and through the general commitment of the staff to a vague multicultural viewpoint'.[19] The school was coming to be seen by outsiders as a model of good multicultural practice. Yet beneath the surface, the head and a few of the more aware teachers were far from content with their multicultural provision and were beginning to feel the need for a planned and co-ordinated policy. Their thoughts were helped to crystallize by a team leader from the local Language Centre and eventually, with the support of two consultants from nearby teacher training institutions, the whole staff decided to embark on a review of their policy and practice. Initial discussions identified a number of 'areas of concern' – the books in the school, the need for knowledge about the school's different cultural groups, the prejudice and attitudes of pupils in the school – which provided the *foci* for small working groups. The task for each group was to 'develop a programme of action and research and keep the other staff informed through large group meetings and reports'. The whole process culminated two terms later in an In-Service Day where detailed reports were woven into a coherent strategy for the future.

Despite obvious differences of scale between this school and the Quinton Kynaston School discussed earlier it is interesting to note some underlying similarities in their methods of working. Both allowed opportunity for a smaller group of staff to follow issues into some depth over a period of time. They stressed the importance of the areas of concern being identified by the teachers themselves. And in both cases structures were established for keeping other members of staff informed of developments. All these seem to be essential elements if a policy is to have the support of those teachers who ultimately will be responsible for enacting it with children.

What is the role of 'experts'?

Of one thing we were sure – that however difficult the task may be, we were not going to accept unthinkingly outside, expert prescription but choose and decide for ourselves. Advice and sympathetic help was welcomed but we were the ones who knew our own children best and who ultimately had to live with the consequences of our choices . . .[20]

Here David Milman sums up the modus vivendi that he and his staff eventually established with those 'experts' on multicultural education whom they called upon for advice in preparing the policy at Childeric

School. Admirable as this self-sufficiency principle may be, however, other teachers have found it more difficult to accept. Atkin and Richards[21] make the perceptive observation that teachers who are unaccustomed to working together on a self-help basis and doubtful of their own capabilities are quite likely to seek security in an 'expert'. This expert could be the headteacher, a scale post holder or, as in the case of Atkin and Richards, some outside authority. Above all, an expert has to be found who will delineate the correct way of proceeding and dispense the necessary knowledge or information. To some degree Atkin and Richards were able to anticipate difficulties of this sort as, from their previous experience of working with teacher groups, they were only too aware of the tendency for consultants to be perceived as experts. At the outset, therefore, they took the decision that they would not accept such a role. Instead, they chose to take on a 'non-directive' facilitating role:

> We wanted to develop a transactional model, in which all that was done was the result of discussion and negotiation, rather than instruction or dictation.[22]

They firmly believed that only through working out their own solutions in a climate of support and constructive comment would the teachers evolve a policy that suited the school and its needs. Appealing as this ideal may seem, however, it is not without its difficulties and our own discussion would be incomplete without some consideration of these difficulties, for they are just as likely to arise for school-based 'experts' – headteachers, deputy head, scale post holders – wishing to adopt the non-directive stance described.

The major difficulty is that teachers do not take willingly to this model of non-directive leadership. This is hardly surprising when one considers that many teachers have been professionally socialized into seeing schools as hierarchical institutions in which headteachers, in consultation with their deputies and senior post-holders, are expected to provide leadership in the traditional sense of making decisions and directing actions. Class teachers may be involved with day-to-day decisions about the work of their pupils but it is usually expected that for guidance on the major aspects of school life they will look to those more prominently placed in the hierarchy. In these circumstances few teachers may have the professional self-confidence to take an active part in decision-making and policy formulation. As a result they may develop a strong sense of dependence towards those whom they perceive as experts. Atkin and Richards discuss this problem as it affected their own roles as consultants:

> The consultants, coming as they did as outsiders, with a role not perhaps clear to the staff, could not escape being invested as the experts with the

'right answers' to the school's perceived needs. Many of the staff, though not all, saw the Working Party as a 'course in multicultural education' where the consultants would impart the latest ideas and practices and they themselves would implement these in their classrooms. The early meetings, therefore, were fraught with tensions, as the consultants demonstrated by their behaviour that this was not the case; there were unspoken questions about what was going on, puzzlement at the perceived lack of leadership from the consultants, anger over the apparent difficulty in deciding what seemed to some staff to be simple matters of tasks and responsibilities.[23]

The tension eventually erupted when one teacher declared: 'we're wasting time. I haven't got time to think, just tell me what to do and I'll get on and do it. Isn't there just one book we could read with all the answers?'[24] It is a problem that does not abate easily and at times the strain can be such that, despite the consultant's conviction that this is the most educationally desirable and professionally effective method of working, he or she may feel inclined to revert to a more authoritarian style. Again, Atkin and Richards make some pertinent observations. They found that with persistence and support for the teachers in learning to work as a group, their approach began to pay dividends. So much so that during the course of the year it was possible to see marked changes in the teachers' group behaviour:

We contrasted one of the last large group meetings where there was lively planning of action and future possibilities with contributions from most members of staff, with the first few meetings where long silences, awkwardness, and no contribution at all from the majority of staff were characteristic. The confidence displayed towards the end of the year represented for us a major shift from dependency to independence, which at best represents a growth in teacher professionalism.[25]

The point I am here trying to make is a simple but fundamental one: although the goal may be to formulate a whole school policy statement on cultural diversity, the zeal for this should not obscure the need to understand that if teachers are to 'own' that policy we should see the issue as part of a longer-term professional development programme designed to equip them to take a more participatory role in decision making and to develop group responsibility for the direction in which the school is travelling.

How to balance priorities?
There are other problems, too, such as time. With any exercise that is concerned with planning for change in schools, time is an important consideration. Despite the best efforts to make time available during the day, in a primary school there is no real alternative but for teachers voluntarily to donate their own personal time after school hours. This

seems to be in the nature of curriculum development. Time, as any primary teacher will acknowledge, is possibly the most scarce resource. Shortage of time is not just a major constraint on the opportunities that teachers have to meet together free from the strains and tensions of the classroom; it also exerts influence on the value which teachers attach to activities that cannot be seen to have an immediate and direct relevance to their classroom work. Of course, ideas of what is 'relevant' and of 'practical value' are highly subjective. But constraints of time can lead to them being applied as criteria for selecting, from among the many competing priorities, those areas with which teachers should concern themselves as part of the policy development process. If this happens, casualties are inevitable and one of the most likely is the teacher's need to reflect upon and evaluate his or her practice. The teacher who asked for the book of answers is not unusual and it is difficult to be without sympathy for her. We must ask ourselves, however, just what would be the consequences of the reflective and evaluative aspects of our work being jettisoned in favour of more tangible and immediately relevant matters. At worst schools would become static and inward looking. At best change would be piecemeal and impulsive, dependent on the whim of individuals. What I am suggesting is that reflection and evaluation should be seen as integral elements of any school's policy formulation work and time priorities should be reviewed to provide opportunity for this to happen.

At the present time many schools are undergoing pressure from their LEAs to clarify their philosophy in relation to issues of race, racism and diversity and to express this in the form of a declared policy. I have already indicated that this, to my mind, is a welcome trend. Unfortunately when it combines with time constraints, and the primary teacher's abiding concern for the practical and the relevant, it can have a deleterious effect on policy planning. Often this issue gives rise to pressure from the teacher for an immediate focusing down on the content aspects of learning: 'What does it mean for me on Monday morning?' One cannot help but be sympathetic, yet a likely result of this 'rush to the tangible' will be lack of time in the early stages of the work for teachers to come to agreement on some fundamental questions about multicultural education. In Chapter 3 the importance of teachers having an understanding of the main concepts of multicultural education was considered. I am suggesting that this discussion should take place during the early orientation phase of the policy building process, since only in doing this can we avoid mistaken assumptions that meanings are shared and held in common. What is more, there are no short cuts. Atkin and Richards put it like this:

It has become clear that . . . development towards a multicultural education approach takes a long time. Pressure of observable 'results' will have precisely the opposite effect of preventing the necessary reflection and reappraisal.[26]

The importance of this continuing process of reflection and reappraisal is further underlined when we recognize that, as a concomitant of teachers having differing personal interpretations of what is meant by a diversity-based approach to learning, they will also occupy different positions on the ideological spectrum. Even within a small primary school, teachers' perspectives on race-related issues may vary greatly. So, at the outset of a policy planning exercise, it will not be unusual to find that one or two teachers have an advanced awareness of the issues involved, have undertaken some initiatives with their own pupils and are working from a clear anti-racist commitment. At the opposite end of the continuum some teachers may have done little or no previous thinking in the area and their general world outlook may lead them intuitively to an assimilationist point of view. Other members of staff may range between the two positions and will be considering the exercise both as a means of furthering their understanding and as a source of support for work in the classroom. In these circumstances pressure for quick observable results would be misguided and, very likely, counterproductive. If the school is to arrive at a corporate statement of purpose time needs to be spent in exploring personal positions, expectations and assumptions. Though challenging and even potentially threatening, this cannot be avoided.

The content of school policies
Earlier in this chapter attention was drawn to two major recommend-ations of the Swann Report.[27] One placed a responsibility on LEAs to request that schools produce policy statements on 'Education For All' and to monitor their implementation. The other urged that schools adopt 'explicit policies to combat racism'. To these we might add a third recommendation:

All schools, whether multi-racial or 'all-white', should review their work in the light of the principles which we have put forward . . .[28]

So it is plain that, as far as the need for policy formulation is concerned, the Report sees no distinction between multicultural schools and those which draw their pupils mainly from the white majority. This should now be our own emphasis as we consider the content of such policies. Unfortunately, when we come to compile case study material it is difficult to find all-white schools that one can include. Many, no doubt, remain to be convinced that they should invest their time and effort in an undertaking that continues to have only peripheral importance for them. Others probably find themselves at a transitional stage between having accepted the case for a policy and being able to translate ideals into words and, then, actuality. Whatever the situation, the net effect is that there is little material on which to draw; but it would be no rationalization to suggest that the experience of multicultural schools will be transferable, albeit with some modification. Similarly, primary schools have much to learn from colleagues at the secondary phase who were generally earlier to recognize the need for the whole-school statement of intent. In discussing policy content I therefore propose adopting the same eclectic approach that has been used in previous chapters.

For some teachers the most pressing priority has been the need for a clear and unequivocal statement of opposition to racism. This is often the case in schools that serve communities where racism is an important local issue, where racist organizations are in evidence and where there have been physical attacks on ethnic minority families. In such circumstances racism is a significant factor in children's day-to-day existence; it will be a major preoccupation for many families and it will find its way into the school both as a topic of conversation among pupils and as an undercurrent to playground and classroom incidents. Faced with such explicit manifestations of racism some schools feel that, for the sake of their relations with pupils and the outside community, they should take a stand. And this stand they see as the lynchpin of their policy. One such school was the Holloway School in North London, to which reference was made earlier. Following increased National Front activity in the neighbourhood and the appearance of a racist leaflet in the school, the headmaster felt it necessary to prepare a staff statement. Included in this was the following set of proposals:

1. We should undertake a campaign of education in assemblies, in lessons and during form periods. Such a campaign should seek to achieve the following:
   a Impress upon the pupils that discrimination against people because of the colour of their skin or place of origin is wrong;
   b Explain why black people, Cypriots and Asians have a right to live in this country. This is particularly important because of the numerous myths that are perpetrated about immigration;
   c Prevent any racialist abuse occurring inside the school wherever we possibly can. For example if epithets like 'coon', 'nigger', 'wog', 'yid', or 'paki' are heard, they should not go unchallenged. We should explain why they are offensive and prevent them from becoming common currency inside the school.

2. The use of materials like films, television programmes, factsheets and stories that assist in the furtherance of the above aims should be encouraged.

3. If any racialist literature appears or is circulated in the school it should be confiscated. Obviously confiscation on its own is not enough; it has to be accompanied by a clear explanation of why we cannot allow the circulation of material that is designed to incite racial animosity and it is clearly dependent on the education programme outlined above. Some may argue that such positive action will create more problems than it will solve. To allow the circulation of such literature in school is an affront to all the black and Cypriot pupils in the school and it would undermine their confidence in the educational system. It would also lead directly to tension and possibly open conflict among the pupils. If any attempts at the circulation of such literature are nipped in the bud it will establish that racist ideas are not 'respectable' and give some credibility to our aims of running a harmonious, multi-racial school.[29]

Examples of other similar statements are to be found in the Swann report.[30] The emphasis in these documents may vary but they all have, as a central plank, an explicit declaration of the school's opposition to racism and an unambiguous set of guidelines on how various types of race-related occurrences should be handled in school. Is such a declaration in itself sufficient, however? No doubt it serves a vital public relations purpose and can do much towards aligning the school with the local community. It leaves pupils in little doubt as to the school's philosophy and thus can help strengthen the morale of ethnic minority children. And the process of drafting and agreeing the statement will be a valuable in-service training experience for staff. But if teachers are to acknowledge the full educational implications of such a stance they will need to have access to more comprehensive guidance, especially in relation to classroom practice – a fact recognized by the Inner London Education Authority in its advice to schools:

Each school or college will finally determine its policy in the light of its own circumstances. However, certain elements are common to all. There will be:

1. A clear, unambiguous statement of opposition to any form of racism or racist behaviour.

2. A firm expression of all pupils' or students' rights to the best possible education.

3. A clear indication of what is not acceptable and the procedures, including sanctions, to deal with any transgressions.

4. An explanation of the way in which the school or college intends to

develop practices which both tackle racism and create educational opportunities which make for a cohesive society and a local school or college community in which diversity can flourish.

5. An outline of the measures by which development will be monitored and evaluated.[31]

We see these broader principles being reflected in the following two statements from primary schools:

The school is multicultural, and all that goes on within it must strive to reflect and build upon this basis.

Culture is central to a child's identity, and the learning environment must reflect the cultures of those learning within it and within society at large.

Teachers must become aware of the cultures from which children come, and the customs and attitudes within them.

Teachers can encourage positive ethnic/cultural self identity by initiating activities which reflect a multicultural society. They should aim to give broad-based information and images about each cultural group, drawing as much as possible from the children's experience in a way that avoids the risk of stereotypes.

Questions about racism, name-calling incidents etc., should never be side-stepped or over responded to. Children should be given appropriate information when and where situations arise. Teachers must avoid the denial of differences that do exist between groups and cultures because these act as a cover for racism.

It is important for teachers to be sensitive to the feelings of parents and children where these relate to cultural conflict.

Teachers must be aware of the racist connotations in language, and avoid such language personally and discourage its use at all times.[32]

1. The pupils at Childeric School come from a variety of cultures, all that goes on should reflect and build on this. Recognition of the school's cultural diversity should also go hand in hand with the recognition of cultures not represented by the school population, including Vietnamese, Greeks, Bengalis and children from travelling families. This should not only take the form of having brown faces on the wall, but there should be recognition of the positive value of mother tongues and dialects. Different languages should be shared and given positive images in the classroom and school generally. Labelling and letters home need to be comprehensible to all children and their families. Differing life styles should be understood and brought out.

2. We must all look at our own prejudices and realise that we see things from a point of view influenced by our own culture, by the media, by what we were taught. We must question the assumptions we make about the children, their families, their environments – are we influenced in our approach by what we think, not what really exists? Class, sex, age, as well as race, come into the sort of judgements we make.

3. We must be aware of the racist connotations in language and avoid such

language personally and discourage its use at all times, e.g. talking about black looks, black marks.

4. We should be aware of stereotyping, whether of class, sex, age or race, and challenge it.

5. We should be aware of the ease with which prejudice can be taught and reinforced.

6. We must encourage positive racial/cultural identity by initiating activities which reflect a multicultural society. We should aim to give information and images about each cultural group, drawing as much as possible from the children's experiences keeping in mind point 4.

7. To extend point 6, the school should make as much contact as possible with parents, community groups and organisations and bodies seeking to encourage and foster aims of multicultural education.

8. Any form of racism should be tackled, never ignored. It should be dealt with by giving the children any appropriate information necessary but care should be taken never to over-respond. There are ethnic differences which cannot be ignored but from children of the age we teach much of the racism is regurgitated from the parents and the children are often ignorant of the significance of what they are saying. This ignorance should not be left uncorrected. Racist remarks from parents should not be ignored either, since inaction can be taken as a sign of agreement. Hopefully once the stance of the school is recognised, then parents will realise it would be inappropriate to voice them. Ancillary staff should be made aware of the non-racist stand the school is making.

9. We must be sensitive to the cultural conflict some parents and children have. We should recognise that to encourage all our children to reach their full potential, they should be helped to fully develop their social growth. All our children should have this opportunity, equally, to be equipped to live harmoniously in our multi-ethnic society.[33]

Again, as with the secondary examples referred to earlier, there are differences of emphasis, but in both cases the specific anti-racist declaration is accompanied by guidance for teachers covering themes such as personal attitudes, behaviour and use of language; the acknowlegement of children's cultural and linguistic skills; the forging of closer links with parents, and responding to community issues. We cannot overestimate the importance of this type of fuller statement since it demonstrates to both teachers and parents that to endorse principles of anti-racism and diversity-based learning entails more than an ideological declaration. It requires, in addition, a reappraisal both of curriculum content and the values and beliefs which underlie teachers' relations with their pupils and the community.

Jon Nixon develops this further by arguing that whatever form a school's policy document takes it should incorporate 'four corner-stones of curriculum planning':

Content, which should reflect the multicultural, multiracial nature of

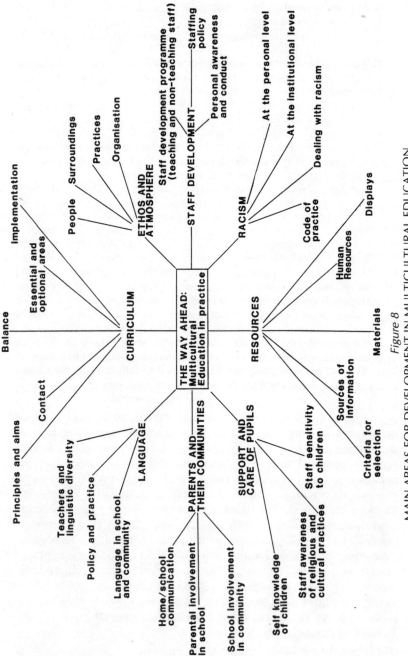

Figure 8

MAIN AREAS FOR DEVELOPMENT IN MULTICULTURAL EDUCATION

British society, past and present.

Styles of teaching, which should be sensitive to the need for both pupils and teachers to enquire beyond their own received assumptions.

Teacher expectations, which should be equally high (in respect of intellectual achievement and social behaviour) for all pupils regardless of cultural background.

Selecting and grouping, which should be free of any bias resulting from the conscious or unconscious stereotyping of particular cultural groups.[34]

The form of the policy document should now be considered. So far, the examples we have quoted have been little more than corporate statements. Indeed, we should acknowledge that the schools concerned would make no greater claims for them than that. In essence, they represent signposts indicating the direction in which the schools intend to travel. Clearly they do not offer the precise guidance necessary if the philosophy they embrace is to take on meaning throughout the school and especially at classroom level. For such precise guidance something more is called for. I therefore want to conclude this discussion of policy content with an example of how a primary school might take the next step of outlining in more detail the implications of its commitment.

The example I have chosen is a document. 'The Way Ahead: Multicultural Education in Practice', prepared by two primary schools in Peterborough.[35] The impetus for this came in March 1983 when the Cambridgeshire LEA issued a statement of policy on 'Race Relations and Education'.[36] For the heads and staff of the two schools this statement was a welcome development but to be of direct value to them in their work it needed to be translated into more specific operational terms. The ensuing two years were devoted to just such an exercise, with a group of teachers from the two schools meeting regularly to make their own interpretation of the LEA's statement. The resulting document is novel for two reasons, first in its comprehensive coverage and, second, in the model it presents of teachers from two schools engaging in a collaborative piece of policy planning. But it is the content aspect with which we are now concerned. Space does not permit us to examine this in detail so, for convenience, I have summarized its main areas in chart form (see Figure 8). Notice the breadth of topics covered – language, curriculum, ethos and atmosphere, staff development, racism, resources, support and care of pupils, parents and community – each of which is broken down into its component parts and then discussed in finer detail, beginning first with an explanation of underlying thinking, and moving on to offer quite specific advice to teachers. Firmly placed within the document is the school's statement on racism. Of necessity this is brief but it contains two essential elements: discussion of how racism can be expected to manifest itself within a school, both at an institutional level and among individuals, and an outline of the steps that teachers themselves can take towards countering it. On the subject of institutional racism the document says the following:

> Institutionalised racism may take the following forms:
> (a) Demeaning of certain individuals by incorrect pronunciation of names and abbreviations of names.
> (b) Low expectations of pupils' roles and abilities.
> (c) Undervaluation of the language and culture of individuals and groups.
> (d) A curriculum which considers only Anglo-Saxon values, norms and attitudes.
> (e) Tests which are based on the achievements of white norms and values.
> (f) Indifference and ignorance of schools to a culture which is not familiar.
> (g) Using resources which either:
>   (i)   reinforce a negative image which is damaging and inaccurate;
>   (ii) ignore the diversity and range of individual differences and customs in our society;
>   (iii) present a warped view of social and economic relations in the world.
> (h) Failure to introduce the necessary machinery for dealing with and responding appropriately to people who are experiencing racism in their day to day existence.
> (i) Under-representation of ethnic minority groups in positions of responsibility.
> (j) Failure to value bilingualism as a prime asset and acknowledge the 'needs' of bilingual pupils.
> (k) Failure to communicate the aims of the school and the value which the school makes of parents who are not fluent in English.
> (l) Unfriendly attitudes to parents.[37]

Notice how each of these themes is set out in quite specific terms which, in turn, lend themselves to translation into curriculum and policy implications. Some, such as (a) 'Demeaning of certain individuals by incorrect pronunciation of names . . .' can provide a focus for a short-term staff development programme involving members of the local communities. Others, like (i) 'Under-representation of ethnic minority groups in positions of responsibility', are less concerned with day-to-day school activities and more with the direction and emphasis of longer term policies and procedures: issues which traditionally have been seen as the concern of headteachers and senior members of staff rather than of classroom practitioners. However, by placing both types of question on the agenda for staff discussion one can help teachers appreciate the complementary relationship between them, whilst developing an overall perspective on the range of themes which should be recognized in a school policy.

This notion of the statement on racism linking directly into classroom practice as well as into discussion of the school's policy priorities is, for me, fundamental if teachers are to be able to conceptualize and act upon the issues which the statement highlights. In other words, when formulating our statements we should be able to demonstrate an awareness of the circumstances in which they will be enacted. The Peterborough document does this very effectively by not only facing racism squarely but also illustrating how the response to racism is firmly within the grasp of those who have responsibility for what happens in the school on a daily basis. Thus the declaration on racism comes to be seen not as a mere ideological stance but as an integral feature of the school's thinking and practice.

Consultation, implementation and monitoring
Having spent some time considering the steps and issues involved in drafting a school policy and determining its content we can now turn to the implementation stage. First, however, there is a period of consultation where the debate is taken beyond those who have been so far directly involved – usually just the teaching staff – and into the wider school community. Prominent here must be the school's governing body. It is often with some trepidation that curriculum issues are taken into that particular forum, especially in schools where the governing body's role is seen in terms of overseeing bricks and mortar rather than involvement with all aspects of children's education. Fortunately, however, this perception is now changing, and with it governors' interests in matters of learning and policy – a development that has certainly been helped by the appointment of more ethnic minority governors and people who are directly involved with the needs of local communities. So the climate among some governing bodies, at least, is now likely to be more welcoming towards participation in curriculum discussions. But even in schools where this is not the case there is just as much reason for dialogue to be initiated, especially as more LEAs begin to draw up policy statements and ask that governors consider the responses that are being made in the schools with which they are associated.

Within the primary school we need to recognize the importance of the secretary, the caretaker, the ancillaries and the dining room staff in determining the ethos within which children learn about questions of race and diversity. As David Milman[38] points out, traditionally their status in the school has been low and their opinions have rarely been considered or valued. Yet these people play a significant part in the life of the school since they often come into close contact with children and parents and frequently act as 'gatekeepers' between the school and the outside world. Some primary schools have involved their non-teaching staff directly in the preparation of the policy. Others, though supporting this idea in principle, feel that in practice difficulties of professional status militate against such collaboration. Nevertheless it is vitally important that, for the policy to be effective, it should be explained to everybody in the school who comes into contact with the pupils and their families. The same can be said for parents. As a minimum step one would hope that through parent governors there would be a channel for regular communication with parents about developments within the school so that even though they may not have been directly involved in drafting the policy, its publication will not come as a surprise to them. But perhaps something more than this is called for if the policy is to have meaning for parents.

At Gayhurst Infants School,[39] Mike Mulvanney and his staff called a meeting with parents specifically to explain the policy. They write:

> When the draft statement was completed by the staff, it was taken to the parents for any discussion and amendment they thought was necessary. Generally they were supportive when each point of the policy was discussed. At the end one parent said, 'It's just as well it was explained to me because I couldn't understand a bloody word of it'. This made us realise that the policy is very jargonistic, and a group of parents and teachers offered to rewrite it in a more understandable form.

Here, we have an example of parents coming to stake a claim in their school's policy. They may not have been directly involved in the policy's initial drafting but, through offering to help rewrite it in a style which they could handle, they have demonstrated plainly to the school that they own it as much as the teachers do. Thus we see emerging the kind of school-community alliance which is so necessary if a policy is to take on life and meaning.

Of course, this process of consultation will not always be straightforward. In almost any school there will be parents with avowedly racist views and others who, at best, are ambivalent about the question of why the school should be concerning itself with issues of race and diversity. Moreover, there are schools where parents have been so vocal as to deter teachers from taking even token steps. Equally, though, there are parents who welcome moves to consultation and whose confidence in the school is enhanced as a result. In these circumstances the task facing teachers must be one of identifying the pockets of support and encouraging the parents involved to take on an educative role within the community at large.

To use the terms 'implementation' and 'monitoring' conjures up for some teachers images of imposition and prescription. They see themselves being required to employ classroom practices and to adopt views for which they have little enthusiasm. No doubt in some cases it will be necessary for a school, once its policy on racism has received majority support, to request all members of staff to view it as a code of conduct governing their professional actions. Furthermore the school may then wish to establish a monitoring procedure whereby teachers' termly forecasts and reports of work are expected to reflect elements of the policy. It may even be necessary to secure the support of the governors and a local inspector in order to implement this. This, however, is not the strategy I would advocate. Indeed, it would be quite out of keeping with the spirit of dialogue and participation which has been stressed on numerous occasions and which is so much a feature of good primary school practice and management. Rather, if the school has followed a procedure where teachers are involved at each stage of the policy planning exercise, the need for a prescriptive approach to implementation need not arise. Recall Patrick Whittaker's advice[40] that it is the teachers themselves who should define 'the problem' and the methods to be used in resolving it. Recall also how his words found an echo in the Swann report[41] where it was stressed that the policy should emerge through teachers reviewing and revising their own practice. With this method of working there need be no abrupt cut-off point between the development and implementation phases. Instead one becomes the natural extension of the other. Similarly with the monitoring elements: if teachers are involved in a cyclical process of action and reflection in the classroom, and if there is a structure whereby the same process can operate at a whole school level, any need for externally imposed sanctions and prescriptions becomes superfluous. In short, the school becomes a place for thinking about, and acting on, multicultural education work in partnership and it is the alliance between these two which is the hallmark of an effective policy.

Summary

In Chapter 6 we have:
1. outlined some of the main arguments for a school policy and summarized the benefits that can accrue;
2. paid close attention to the process of formulating a policy, addressing specific questions about who should be involved, the methods of working to be used, the role of 'experts', and how to cope with competing priorities;

References

Chapter 1 pages 9–29
1 This extract is taken from Barbara Roberts's contribution to programme 2 ('A Primary Response') of the BBC TV series 'Case Studies in Multicultural Education'. In the programme she is seen working on themes concerning 'migration' and 'ourselves' wit⁴ her class of older juniors at Ecklesbourne primary school in North London.
2 This is extracted from programme 1 ('Anglo-Saxon Attitudes') of the same series. This section of the film focuses on an exchange project involving Shaftesbury, a multicultural junior school in inner Leicester, and Newbold Verbold Primary School on the city's outskirts.
3 Swann, M. (1985) *Education for All*, p. 319, HMSO.
4 For a fuller treatment see, Holmes, C. (1978) ed. *Immigrants and Minorities in Britain*, Allen and Unwin.
5 For readers unfamiliar with this aspect of the language debate see Giles, H. and Johnson, P. 'The role of language in ethnic group relations', in Turner and Giles (1981), *Intergroup Behaviour*, Basil Blackwell.
6 Price, G. (1984), *The Languages of Britain*, Edward Arnold.
7 Lockwood, W. B. (1975), *The Languages of the British Isles Past and Present*, Andre Deutsch.
8 Price, G. op. cit.
9 Llewelyn, R. (1939) *How Green Was My Valley*, pp. 319–20, Michael Joseph.
10 Both Price, op. cit. and Lockwood, op. cit. contain informative sections on the history of the Irish language.
11 Price, op. cit.
12 McKinnon, K. (1978), *Gaelic in Scotland, 1971: some sociological and demographic considerations of the Census Report for Gaelic*, Hatfield Polytechnic.
13 Nance, M. (1973) 'When was Cornish last spoken traditionally?', *Journal of the Royal Institution of Cornwall*, 7:76–82.
14 Fuere, S. (1978) *Britannia: A History of Roman Britain*, Routledge and Kegan Paul.
15 See: Baugh, A. C. and Cable, T. (1978) *A History of the English Language*, Routledge and Kegan Paul, pp. 93–100. They estimate that 'more than 1,400 places in England bear Scandinavian place names'. More than 600 have the -by (farm) ending (Whitby, Derby, etc); 300 have the -thorp/e (village) ending (Athorp, Linthorpe); 300 end in -thwaite (isolated land) (Applethwaite, Braithwaite). They also note how medieval records of these places often show families with names ending in the Scandinavian -son (Stevenson, Johnson).
16 Brand, Rev. J. (1700) cited in Price, op. cit.
17 MacKenzie, M. (1750) cited in Price, op. cit.
18 Orr, J. (1948) *The impact of French upon English*, Clarendon Press, Oxford.
19 Baugh, A. C. and Cable, T., op. cit.
20 Kellenbenz, H. (1978) 'German immigrants in England', in Holmes, C. (1978) ed. *Immigrants and Minorities in British Society*, Allen and Unwin.

21 Kiernan, V. G. (1978) 'Britons old and new', in Holmes, C., ibid.
22 Acton, T. (1974), *Gypsy Politics and Social Change*, Routledge and Kegan Paul.
23 Kenrick, D. (1979) 'Romani English', *International Journal of the Sociology of Language*, 19:111–120.
24 Acton, T. and Davis, G. (1979) 'Educational policy and language use among English Romanies and Irish travellers in England and Wales', *International Journal of the Sociology of Language*, 19:91–109.
25 Fryer, P. (1984) *Staying Power -- the history of black people in Britain*, Pluto.
26 Hakluyt, R. 'The Second Voyage of John Lake, 1554–5', in 'The Principal Navigations, Voiages, Traffiques and Discoveries of the English', 1904 edn., Vol. VI. Cited in File, N. and Power, C. (1981) *Black Settlers in Britain, 1555–1958*, Heinemann.
27 Hughes, J. L. and Larkin, J. F., eds. (1969) 'Licensing Caspar Van Sanden to deport negroes', in *Tudor Royal Proclamations, 1588–1603*.
28 File, N. and Power, C., op. cit.
29 *The Gentleman's Magazine*, Vol. 34, 1763, p. 493. Cited in File, N. and Power, C., op. cit.
30 Ibid.
31 *The Morning Post*, December 22, 1786. Cited in File, N. and Power, C., op. cit.
32 Fryer, P., op. cit.
33 File, N. and Power, C., op. cit.
34 Gordon, J. E. (1975) 'Mary Seacole – a forgotten nurse. Heroine of the Crimea', *The Midwife, Health Visitor and Community Nurse*, Vol. ii, February.
35 This theme is explored well by Fryer, op. cit. and File and Power, op. cit.
36 Visram, R. and Dewjee, A. (1984) 'Dadabhai Nairoji: Britain's First Black M.P.', *Dragon's Teeth*, No. 17, Spring.
37 See Little, K. L. (1947) *Negroes in Britain*, Routledge and Kegan Paul.
38 Karaka, D. F. *This Your England*, Cited in Hiro, D (1971) *Black British, White British*, Pelican
39 'Struggle for Black Community: Tiger Bay is my home', (1984), ITV Channel 4, 15 August.
40 Ibid.
41 Ibid.
42 Ibid.
43 Ibid.
44 Ibid.
45 See DES (1983) *Memorandum on Compliance with Directive 77/486 EC on the Education of Children of Migrant Workers*, February.
46 Tansley, P. et al (1986) *Community languages in the primary school*, NFER Nelson.
47 *The Children's Language Project* (1984), Philip and Tacey.
48 Ibid.
49 Tansley, P. and Craft, A. (1984) 'Mother Tongue Teaching and Support: A Schools Council Enquiry'. *Journal of Multilingual and Multicultural Development*, 5, pp. 367–84.
50 The term 'bilingual' here refers to children who speak a home language other than English and who are at some stage in learning English as a Second Language.
51 Rosen, H. and Burgess, T. (1980) *Languages and Dialects of London School Children*, Ward Lock Educational.
52 ILEA (1983) *The 1983 Language Census*, ILEA 3573.
53 See Schools Council Mother Tongue Project (1984) *Papers presented to the European Commission Colloquium*, School Curriculum Development Project.
54 Linguistic Minorities Project (1983) *Linguistic Minorities in England: a report to the Dept. of Education and Science*, July, Tinga Tinga/Heinemann.
55 Tansley, P. et al, op. cit.
56 Davis, G. (1982) 'Multicultural Education: some assumptions underlying current practices', *Multi-Ethnic Education Review*, Vol. 1, No. 2. Summer.

57 Hussey, M. (1982) 'Education in a Multi-ethnic Society', *Multi-Ethnic Education Review*. Vol. 1, No. 2, Summer.
58 Swann, M. op. cit., p. 319.
59 DES (1975) *A Language for Life*, para 20.5, HMSO.
60 Swann, M., op. cit., Chapter 6.
61 Davis, G., op. cit.
62 House of Commons Home Affairs Committee (1981), *Fifth Report: Racial Disadvantage*, Vol. 1, para 155, HMSO.
63 Rushdie, S. (1982) 'The New Empire Within Britain', *The Listener*, 9 November.
64 Lynch, J. (1983) *The Multicultural Curriculum*, p. 44, Batsford.
65 Although I, myself, have reservations about the use of the term 'basic' in relation to Mathematics and English I have employed it here because it is still in widespread use among primary teachers. See for instance 'Back to Basics? We've Never Left Them'. *Times Educational Supplement*, 7 December 1984.
66 Houlton, D. (1984) 'Responding to Diversity'. *Multicultural Teaching*, Vol. 11, No. 3, Summer.
67 Lynch, J., op. cit. p. 45. See also Willey, R. (1982) *Teaching in Multicultural Britain*, Longman for the Schools Council.
68 Little, A. and Willey, R. (1981) '*Multi-Ethnic Education: the way forward*', p. 20, Schools Council.
69 *Education for a Multiracial Society – Curriculum and Context 5–13* (1981) Schools Council.
70 The chapter dealing with these themes was not published in the main report but was later printed in *New Society* as 'Race and Teachers, The Schools Council Study', 16 February 1978.
71 The term 'anti-racist teaching' has been in use for some time and it is difficult to identify its origins but one of its more prominent exponents is Chris Mullard of the London Institute of Education. See, for instance, Mullard, C. (1982) 'Multiracial Education in Britain: from assimilation to cultural pluralism', in Tierney, J., ed., *Race, Migration and Schooling*, Holt Saunders.
72 The term 'education for racial equality' is particularly associated with the pioneering policy of the Berkshire LEA. See, *Education for Racial Equality: policy paper 1*, issued by the Director of Education, Shire Hall, Reading, RG2 9XE.
73 Swann, op. cit. p. 320.
74 Craft, A. and Klein, G. (1986) *Agenda for Multicultural Teaching*, Longman for the School Curriculum Development Committee.

Chapter 2 pages 30–49

1 I am here referring to the teachers from Newbold Verdon primary school whose work was described in Chapter 1.
2 The Schools Council Mother Tongue Project ran between May 1981 and August 1985. It was concerned with preparing resources for use by teachers in supporting the bilingualism of primary age children. Further details of the project can be obtained from: The Information Section, School Curriculum Development Committee, Newcombe House, Notting Hill Gate, London W11 3JB.
3 Quoted in Houlton, D. (1985) *All Our Languages*, Edward Arnold.
4 See, in particular, Linguistic Minorities Project (1983) *Linguistic Minorities in England*, Tinga Tinga/Heinemann, July.
5 Ibid.
6 Saifullah Khan, V. (1976) 'Provision by minorities for language maintenance', in *Bilingualism and British Education: the dimensions of diversity*, Centre for Information on Language Teaching and Research.
7 Linguistic Minorities Project, op. cit.
8 Mercer, L. (1981) 'Ethnicity and the Supplementary School', in Mercer, N. (1981), ed., *Language in School and Community*, Edward Arnold.

9 ibid.
10 Fishman, J. A. and Nahirny, V. C. (1966) 'The ethnic group school and mother tongue maintenance', in Fishman, J. A., ed., *Language loyalty in the United States*, Mouton, The Hague.
11 Mercer, L., op. cit.
12 ibid.
13 Kingston, M. H. (1981), *The Woman Warrior*, Picador.
14 ibid.
15 See Wilson, A. (1978) *Finding A Voice: Asian women in Britain*, Virago.
16 Miller, J. (1983) *Many Voices: Bilingualism, Culture and Education*, Routledge and Kegan Paul.
17 ibid.
18 Weinreich, U. (1953) *Languages in Contact: Findings and Problems*, Mouton (2nd edn. 1979).
19 ibid.
20 See Richards, J. C., ed., (1974) *Error Analysis: Perspectives on Second Language Acquisition*, Longman.
21 This is a theme taken up in Giles, H. and Johnson, P. (1981) 'The Role of Language in Ethnic Group Relations' in Turner and Giles, eds., *Intergroup Behaviour*, Blackwell.
22 Miller, J., op. cit.
23 ibid.
24 Sluckin, A. (1981), *Growing up in the Playground: the social development of children*, Routledge and Kegan Paul.
25 Opie, I. and Opie, P. (1977) *The Lore and Language of Schoolchildren*, Paladin.
26 I use the term 'indigenous' in the full knowledge that it is becoming increasingly inappropriate as a means of differentiating between those children who have their cultural roots in Britain and those whose origins lie elsewhere in the world.
27 Wilson, A., op. cit.
28 Rosen, H. and Burgess, T. (1981) *Languages and Dialects of London Schoolchildren*, Ward Lock Educational.
29 The materials from this project were eventually published as *World in a City*, by the Inner London Education Authority and the Commission for Racial Equality.
30 Wright, J. (1983) 'Different but Equal', *Times Educational Supplement*, 30 September.
31 ibid.
32 Davey, A. (1983) *Learning to be Prejudiced*, Edward Arnold.
33 Milner, D. (1983) *Children and Race, Ten Years On*, Ward Lock Educational.
34 Cohen, L. and Manion, L. (1983) *Multicultural Classrooms*, Croom Helm.
35 Horowitz, E. L. (1936) 'Development of attitudes towards Negroes', *Archives of Psychology*, No. 194.
36 Clark, K. and Clark, M. (1939) 'The development of consciousness of self and the emergence of racial identification in Negro pre-school children', *Journal of Social Psychology*, SSPI Bulletin 10.
37 Goodman, M. (1952) *Race Awareness in Young Children*, Addison-Wesley.
38 Milner, D., op. cit.
39 In the studies mentioned the term 'black' was used specifically to describe children of Afro-American/Afro-Caribbean origin. But henceforth I shall use it as a generic term to include South Asians and Afro-Caribbeans.
40 See Simmons, R. G. (1978) 'Blacks and high self-esteem: a puzzle', *Social Psychology*, 41.
41 See Davey, A. G. and Mullin, P. N. (1982) 'Inter-ethnic friendship in British primary schools', *Educational Research*, 24, 2.
42 Milner, D., op. cit.
43 Stone, M. (1981) *The Education of the Black Child in Britain: the myth of multiracial education*, Fontana.

44 See, for instance, Nixon, J. (1985) *A Teacher's Guide to Multicultural Education*, Blackwell.
45 Swann, M., op. cit., p. 35.
46 For a fuller treatment of this see Jeffcoate, R. (1977) 'Children's Racial Ideas and Feelings', *English in Education*, 11(1).
47 Goodman, M., op. cit.
48 Marsh, A. (1970) 'Awareness of Racial Differences in West African and British Children', *Race XI*, No. 3.
49 Goodman, M. (1964) *Race Awareness in Young Children*, Collier.
50 See Milner's discussion of the work of Katz which is based on a more detailed set of cognitive categories: Milner, op. cit., Chapter 5.
51 See Milner, op. cit., Chapter 5, for more details of these studies.
52 Morland, J. K. (1963) 'Racial self-identification: a study of nursery school children', *American Catholic Sociological Review*, 24.
53 Clark, K. (1955) *Prejudice and Your Child*, Beacon Press.
54 Milner, D., op. cit., Chapter 5.
55 ibid.
56 ibid.
57 ibid.
58 Rowley, K. G. (1968) 'Social Relations Between British and Immigrant Children', *Educational Research*, 10.
59 Kawwa, T. (1968) 'Three Sociometric Studies of Ethnic Relations in London Schools', *Race 10* (2).
60 Durojaiye, M. O. A. (1970) 'Patterns of Friendship Choices in an Ethnically-mixed Junior School', *Race*, 12.
61 Jelinek, M. M. and Brittan, E. M. (1975) 'Multiracial Education: 1. Inter-ethnic Friendship Patterns', *Educational Research*, 18(1).
62 Swann, M., op. cit., pp. 251–2.
63 ibid. p. 35.
64 ibid.
65 ibid.
66 Forsythe, J. (1983) 'Sleep in Peace Now, the battle's o'er', *New Internationalist*, No. 128, October.
67 ibid.
68 Giles, H. and Powerland, P. (1975) *Speech Style and Social Evaluations*, Academic Press.
69 Edwards, V. (1983) *Language in Multicultural Classrooms*, Chapter 5, Batsford Academic.
70 Quoted in Edwards, ibid.
71 Quoted in Edwards, ibid.
72 Bernstein, B. (1973) *Class, Codes and Control*, Vol. 1, Routledge and Kegan Paul.
73 Edwards, V., op. cit.
74 Midwinter, E. (1972) *Priority Education*, Penguin.
75 Labov, W. (1969) *The Logic of Non-Standard English*, Georgetown University Monograph Series Vol. 22.
76 Rosen, H. (1976) *Language and Class: a critical look at the theories of Basil Bernstein*, Falling Wall Press.
77 Houston, S. H. (1970) 'A Re-examination of Some Assumptions about the Language of the Disadvantaged Child', *Child Development*, 41.
78 DES (1975) *A Language for Life*, HMSO, para 20.5.
79 McLeod, A. (1982) 'Writing, Dialect and Linguistic Awareness' in Talk Workshop Group (1982) *Becoming Our Own Experts: The Vauxhall Papers*.
80 Goodman, K. and Buck, C. (1973) 'Dialect barriers to reading comprehension revisited', *The Reading Teacher*, 27.
81 Berdan, R. (1981) *'Black English and dialect-fair instruction'*, in Mercer, N., ed., op. cit.

82 ibid.
83 ibid.
84 ibid.
85 ibid.
86 Studdert, J. and Wiles, S. (1982) *Children's Writing in the Multilingual Classroom*, Centre for Urban Educational Studies Occasional Papers, ILEA.
87 Edwards, V., op. cit.
88 See: Richmond, J. (1979) 'Dialect features in mainstream school writing', *New Approaches to Multiracial Education*, 8(1).
89 Swann, M., op. cit.
90 Edwards, V., op. cit., Chap. 8.

Chapter 3 pages 50–77
 1 Rosenthal, R. and Jacobson, L. (1968) *Pygmalion in the Classroom*, Holt, Rinehart and Winston.
 2 See, for example, Thorndike, R. L. (1968), review of R. Rosenthal and L. Jacobson, *Pygmalion in the Classroom*, *American Educational Research Journal*, 5, 708–11: and Shipman, M. (1975), *Limitations of Social Research*, Longman.
 3 Rist, R. C. (1970), 'Student Social Class and Teacher Expectations: the self-fulfilling prophecy in ghetto education', *Harvard Educational Review*, Vol. 40, No. 3, August.
 4 Rubovitz, P. C. and Maehr, M. L. (1973), 'Pygmalion Black and White', *Journal of Personality and Social Psychology*, 25, 2, 210–18.
 5 Rosenthal, R. (1973), 'The Pygmalion effect lives', *Psychology Today*, 1, 58–63.
 6 See Peter Green's paper, *Multi-Ethnic Teaching and the Pupils' Self-Concept*, Annex B of Chapter 2 of the Swann Report.
 7 Short, G. (1985), 'Teacher Expectation and West Indian Underachievement', *Educational Research*, Vol. 27, Number 2, June.
 8 See Chapter 3 of the Swann Report, 'Achievement and Underachievement'.
 9 Brittan, E. M. (1976), 'Multiracial Education 2. Teacher opinion on aspects of school life. Part One: changes in curriculum and school organization', *Educational Research*, Vol. 18, No. 2, 96–116.
10 Little, A. and Willey, R. (1983) *Studies in the Multi-ethnic Curriculum*, Schools Council.
11 The background to the Fallows and Matthews studies is discussed in Chapter 5 of the Swann Report, 'Multicultural Education: Further Research Studies', 3. 1–3.5.
12 Swann, op. cit., Chapter 5, Annexes C and D.
13 ibid., Chapter 5, 3.3.
14 ibid.
15 ibid.
16 ibid.
17 Gay, G. (1981) 'Multiculturalizing Teacher Education', *Urban Education*, Vol. 5, No. 2, Winter, pp. 12–20.
18 Davis, G. (1982), 'Multicultural Education: some assumptions underlying current practices', *Multi-Ethnic Education Review*, Vol. 1.1, No. 2, Summer.
19 James, A. (1980) *Ideologies in Multicultural Education*. Unpublished manuscript quoted in the Open University course E354, block 4.
20 This chart arises from in-service work in Berkshire LEA. A fuller discussion of it is to be found in Richardson, R. (1985), 'Punch and the Devil', *New Internationalist*, March.
21 Richmond, J. (1982) 'Talking and Writing – Connections? – an Instance', in *Becoming Our Own Experts*, ILEA English Centre.
22 Adelman, C. et al (1983) *A Fair Hearing for All: relationships between teaching and racial equality*, Bulmershe College of Higher Education, Reading.
23 One of the most comprehensive publication guides, covering all aspects of

multicultural education, is Gillian Klein's *Resources for Multicultural Education*, Schools Council (1982).

24 Gay, G., op. cit.

25 Gay, G., ibid.

26 Gay, G. (1985) 'Teacher Education for a Multicultural Society', unpublished paper, University of Nottingham, May.

27 BBC-TV (1981) 'School Report', programme 5 in the series 'Case Studies in Multicultural Education', Autumn.

28 BBC-TV, ibid.

29 Schools Council (1983) *Nottingham University Family Lifestyles Pack*, Nottingham University School of Education.

30 Schools Council, ibid.

31 Gay, G., op. cit.

32 The case for using discussion techniques in multicultural education is presented well in Richardson, R. (1982) 'Talking about equality: the use and importance of discussion in multicultural education', Cambridge Journal of Education 12(2): 101–114.

33 Gay, G., op. cit.

34 Schools Council, op. cit.

35 Thomas, K. (1985) 'The Multicultural Society: some curricular implications', in Day et al, ed., *Prospect for Curriculum: purpose, provision and practice*, Association for Study of the Curriculum.

36 Katz, J. (1978) *White Awareness: handbook for anti-racism training*, University of Oklahoma Press.

37 Reference has already been made to specific programmes in the series, but the series itself comprises ten 25 minute in-service training films for teachers produced by the BBC Continuing Education Dept. The handbook accompanying the programmes is *Multicultural Education*, by John Twitchin and Clare Demuth (BBC Publications).

38 Twitchin, J. and Demuth, C., op. cit.

39 ibid.

40 ibid.

41 ibid.

42 Schools Council (1981), *Education for a Multiracial Society: Curriculum and Context 5–13*.

43 ibid.

44 For a discussion of this issue see Galton, M. and Simon, B. (1980). *Progress and Performance in the Primary Classroom (Observational Research and Classroom Learning)*, Routledge and Kegan Paul.

45 Rowland, S. (1984) 'What is really meant by – the teacher as co-learner?', *Dialogue in Education*, Vol. 1, No. 1, Autumn.

46 ibid.

47 Barnes, D. and Todd, F. (1977) *Communication and Learning in Small Groups*, Routledge and Kegan Paul.

48 ibid.

49 ibid.

50 See, for example, Stubbs, M. (1976) *Language, Schools and Classrooms*, Methuen.

51 The Berkshire LEA has produced three papers dealing with different aspects of its policy, 'Education for Racial Equality'. The checklist mentioned is contained in paper 2, 'Implications'. The other papers are: paper 1, 'General Policy', paper 3, 'Support'.

52 The three policy papers are reproduced as Annex A to Chapter 6 of the Swann Report.

Chapter 4 pages 78–100

1 Plowden Report (1967) *Children and their Primary Schools*, HMSO.

170   References

2 See McGeeney, P. (1969) *Parents are Welcome*, Longman.
3 See Bernstein, B. and Davis, A. (1969) 'Some Sociological Comments on Plowden', in Peters, R. S., ed., *Perspectives on Plowden*, Routledge and Kegan Paul.
4 Newson, J. and Newson, E. (1977) *Perspectives on School at Seven Years Old*, George Allen and Unwin.
5 Tizard, B. et al (1981) *Involving Parents in Nursery and Infant Schools*, Grant McIntyre.
6 Wells, G. (1981) *Learning through Interaction*, Cambridge University Press.
7 Cyster, R., Clift, P. S. and Battle, S. (1979) *Parental Involvement in Primary Schools*, NFER.
8 See Cyster, R. and Clift, P. (1980) 'Parental Involvement in Primary Schools: the NFER survey', in Craft, M. et al, ed., *Linking Home and School*, 3rd ed., Harper and Row.
9 See Tomlinson, S. (1980) 'Ethnic Minority Parents and Education', in Craft, M. et al, ibid.
10 ibid.
11 Ghuman, P. A. S. (1980) 'Punjabi Parents and English Education', *Education Research*, Vol. 22, No. 2. pp. 121–30.
12 Reported in Tomlinson, S. (1984) *Home and School in Multicultural Britain*, Batsford Academic, Chapter 4.
13 See Swann, M. (1985) *Education for All*, HMSO, Chapter 4, Annex A.
14 Stone, M. (1981) *The Education of the Black Child in Britain: the Myth of Multiracial Education*, Fontana.
15 ibid., Chapter 4.
16 Fulloway, C. (1985) *Parents, Teachers, Children*. Unpublished dissertation, University of Nottingham.
17 Education Act (1980), HMSO.
18 Bastiani, J. (1978), *Written Communication Between Home and School*, University of Nottingham.
19 For a fuller treatment of the practical issues involved in establishing bilingual communication between home and school, see Houlton, D. (1985), *All Our Languages*, Edward Arnold.
20 Houlton, D., ibid., p. 41.
21 ibid, p. 42.
22 ibid, p. 43.
23 ibid, p. 44.
24 See, for example, Sharrock, A. (1970), 'Aspects of Communication Between School and Parent', *Journal of Educational Research*, Vol. 10, No. 3; and Daynes, R. W. (1977), 'Towards Effective Teacher Parent Contact', unpublished dissertation, University of Sussex.
25 See Tomlinson, S. (1980) 'Ethnic Minority Parents and Education' in Craft, M. et al, ed., *Linking Home and School*, 3rd ed., Harper and Row.
26 Tomlinson, S., ibid.
27 Nixon, J. (1985) *A Teacher's Guide to Multicultural Education*, Basil Blackwell, Chapter 7.
28 For a fuller discussion of this idea see Bastiani, J. (1983), *Listening to Parents*, unpublished Ph. D. dissertation, University of Nottingham.
29 DES (1981) *West Indian Children in Our Schools: A Report of the Committee of Enquiry into the Education of Children from Ethnic Minority Groups*, HMSO, p. 80.
30 Barron, G. and Howell, D. (1974), *The Government and Management of Schools*, Athlone Press.
31 Tomlinson, S. (1984) *Home and School in Multicultural Britain*, Batsford.
32 Houlton, D. (1985) op. cit., p. 48.
33 For a discussion of this see Aplin, G. and Pugh, G. (1983), *Perspectives on Pre-school Visiting*, National Children's Bureau.

34 Tomlinson, S. (1984) op. cit.
35 See, for example, Yates, O. (1982) *Final Report of the Van Leer/Open University Project on Parenting Materials*, unpublished Report for Birmingham LEA.
36 Tizard, B. and Hughes, M. (1984) *Young Children Learning: talking and thinking at home and school*, Fontana.
37 See, for example, Fairbairn, A. N. (1971) *The Leicestershire Community Colleges*, National Institute of Adult Education.
38 Midwinter, E. (1972) *Priority–Education*, Penguin.
39 Houlton, D. and Willey, R. (1983) *Supporting Children's Bilingualism*, Longman/Schools Council.
40 Nixon, J. (1985) op. cit.
41 AFFOR (1982), *Talking Chalk: Black Pupils, Parents and Teachers Speak about Education*, Birmingham: AFFOR (All Faiths For One Race), p. 38.
42 Tomlinson, S. (1984) op. cit., Chapter 6.
43 Twitchin, J. and Demuth, C. (1981) *Multicultural Education: views from the classroom*, BBC.
44 ibid.
45 Houlton, D. (1985) op. cit., p. 46.
46 Richards, K. (1983) 'A Contribution to the Multicultural Education Debate', *New Community*, Vol. 10, No. 2, pp. 222–5.
47 Newson, J. and Newson, E. (1977) op. cit.
48 Hewison, J. and Tizard, J. (1980) 'Parental Involvement and Reading Attainment', *British Journal of Educational Psychology*, Vol. 50, pp. 209–15.
49 Jackson, A. and Hannon, P. (1981) *The Bellfield Reading Project*, Bellfield Community Council, Rochdale.
50 Widlake, P. and Macleod, F. (1984) *Rising Standards*, Community Education Development Centre, Coventry.
51 Hamilton, D. and Griffiths, A. (1984) *Parent, Teacher, Child*, Methuen.

Chapter 5 pages 101–140
1 Berkshire County Council (1983) *Education for Racial Equality: policy paper 2. 'Implications'*.
2 Inner London Education Authority (1981) *Education in a Multi-Ethnic Society – An aide memoire for the Inspectorate*.
3 Quoted in Houlton, D. (1985) *All Our Languages: A Handbook for the Multilingual Classroom*, Edward Arnold.
4 ibid.
5 Rowland, S. (1984) 'What is really meant by – the teacher as co-learner?', *Dialogue in Education*, Vol. 1, No. 1. Autumn.
6 DES (1978) *Primary Education in England*, HMSO, para. 3, p. 19.
7 Rowland, op. cit.
8 ibid.
9 ibid.
10 ibid.
11 The Language in the Multicultural Primary Classroom Project (LMPC) was sponsored by the Schools Council and ran between 1982 and 1984. It was directed by Hilary Hester. Further information can be obtained from the Information Section, School Curriculum Development Committee, Newcombe House, 45 Notting Hill Gate, London W11 3JB.
12 Language in the Multicultural Primary Classroom Project (1982) *Broadsheet 2: Work in progress*, Schools Council Publications.
13 ibid.
14 For a fuller treatment of classroom discourse see Sinclair, J. and Coulthard, M. (1975) *Towards an Analysis of Discourse: The English used by teachers and pupils*, Oxford University Press.

15 Rogers, C. (1983) *Freedom to Learn for the 80s*, Charles, E. Merrill/Bell and Howell.
16 Glass, V. (1975) 'The Wendy House in the Multi-racial Classroom', *Change – the Newsletter of the Leicestershire Branch of NAME*, January.
17 Hemmings, R. (1980) 'Multi-ethnic Mathematics', *New Approaches in Multiracial Education*, Vol. 8, No. 3, Summer.
18 Quoted in Houlton, D. (1985) op. cit.
19 ibid.
20 ibid.
21 This is based on the topic web idea described in Richardson, R., Flood, M. and Fisher, S. (1981) *Debate and Decision: schools in a world of change*, World Studies Project.
22 Alexandra Infant School, Haringey (1984) *Spinning Tops From Around the World*, Reading Matters Community Bookshop, 10 Lymington Avenue, London N22.
23 Sachdeva, S. (1985), Games, in *Language Two: Classroom initiatives to support language diversity*, Leicester Bilingual Support Group, Rushey Mead Centre, Harrison Road, Leicester.
24 This is extracted from 'A Primary Response', programme 2 in the BBC-TV series *Case Studies in Multicultural Education*.
25 Linda Cushine's account of her work appears in Gregory, A. and Woollard, N. (1984) *Looking in Language: diversity in the classroom*, Berkshire Support Service for Language and Intercultural Education.
26 *Children's Language Project* (1984), Philip and Tacey Ltd.
27 This example is extracted from 'A Primary Response', programme 2 in the BBC-TV series quoted above, note 24.
28 The full text of Martin Francis's interview for the BBC-TV programme appears in Twitchin, J. and Demuth, C. (1981) *Multicultural Education: views from the classroom*, BBC Publications.
29 The *Tomorrow's People* series was broadcast by Yorkshire Television.
30 Language in the Multicultural Primary Classroom Project (1983) *Broadsheet. Work in Progress C. Names, name-calling . . .*, Schools Council Publications.
31 See, for example, Smith, B. and Rhymes, H. (1983) 'Letters from Strangers: Talking to Friends', *Multicultural Teaching*, Vol. 1, No. 3. Summer.
32 Houlton, D. and Houlton, S. (1975) *Getting Together*, Leicestershire NAME.
33 See, for example, 'Anglo-Saxon Attitudes', programme 1 in the BBC-TV series mentioned above, note 24.
34 Fitch, D. (1984) 'Catching Crabs at the Seaside', *Multicultural Teaching*, Vol. 11, No. 3, Summer.
35 Bochner, S. (1982) *Cultures in Contact*, Pergamon. Quoted in Fitch, ibid.
36 ibid.
37 Twitchin, J. and Demuth, C., op. cit.
38 Green, J. (1984) 'Education for a multicultural society', *Primary Education Newsletter*, No. 28, Autumn, University of Nottingham.
39 See Schools Council (1971) *Social Studies 8–13: a report of the middle years of schooling*, Evans.

Chapter 6 pages 141–162
 1 Leicestershire LEA (1984) *Report of the Working Party on Multicultural Education*, December.
 2 ibid., page 4, paragraph 11.
 3 Swann, M. (1985) *Education for All*, Chapter 6, paragraph 4.8.
 4 ibid, paragraph 4.18.
 5 ibid., paragraph 4.10.
 6 Twitchin, J. and Demuth, C. (1981) *Multicultural Education: Views from the classroom*, Chapter 10.
 7 Mulvanney, M. (1984) 'The impact of an anti-racist policy in the school community',

in Straker-Welds, M., ed., *Education for a Multicultural Society: Case studies in ILEA schools*, Bell and Hyman.

8 Milman, D. (1984) 'Childeric School: Developing a Multicultural Policy', in Straker-Welds, ibid.

9 Inner London Education Authority (1983) *Race, Sex and Class, 2: Multi-Ethnic Education in Schools*, pp. 24–5.

10 Whitaker, P. (1983) *The Primary Head*, Heinemann, pp. 54–55.

11 ibid.

12 National Union of Teachers (1982) *Education for a Multicultural Society: Evidence to the Swann Committee of Inquiry*.

13 Swann M., op. cit., Chapter 5, paragraph 4.8.

14 ibid.

15 Mitchell, P. (1982) 'Developing an Anti-racist policy', *Multi-Ethnic Education Review*, Vol. 1, No. 2, Summer.

16 This is an issue which greatly concerned the staff of Birley High School in Manchester and is treated in some detail in their report: Birley High School (1980) *Multicultural Education in the 1980's, Report of a working party of teachers at Birley High School, Manchester*.

17 Atkin, J. and Richards, K. (1983) *A Question of Priorities: an examination of a school-based inservice education programme in multicultural education*, University of Nottingham.

18 ibid., p. 2.

19 ibid., p. 2.

20 Milman, D., op. cit.

21 Atkin, J. and Richards, K., op. cit., page 3.

22 ibid., p. 3.

23 ibid., p. 17.

24 ibid., p. 17.

25 ibid., p. 18.

26 ibid., p. 27.

27 Swann, op. cit., paragraphs 4.18., 4.10.

28 Swann, M., op. cit., p. 365.

29 Twitchin, J. and Demuth, C., op. cit., pp. 109–10.

30 See Swann, M., op. cit., pp. 380–81.

31 Inner London Education Authority, op. cit., p. 25.

32 Mulvanney, M., op. cit.

33 From Milman, D., op. cit.

34 Nixon, J. (1985) *A Teacher's Guide to Multicultural Education*, Blackwell, p. 50.

35 Cambridge Education Committee (1985) *The Way Ahead: Multicultural Education in Practice*. This document was prepared by the Headteachers and staff of the Beeches and the Gladstone Primary Schools in Peterborough.

36 Cambridgeshire County Council (1983) *Race Relations and Education: A Statement of Policy*.

37 Cambridgeshire Education Committee, op. cit.

38 Milman, D., op. cit., p. 39.

39 Mulvanney, M., op. cit. p. 29.

40 Whitaker, P., op. cit.

41 Swann, M., op. cit., Chapter 6 para. 4.8.

Index